THE GREAT LEEL

THE GREAT LEEDS PUB CRAWL

Simon Jenkins

Scratching Shed Publishing Ltd

Cover: The main image is courtesy of North Bar Group.
The images of the Reliance, front right and on the spine, are
courtesy of Yorkshire Post Newspapers. The Griffin (left)
and Hop (centre) are by the author. On the rear, the images
of Whitelock's (rear above) and Garden Gate (below right)
are by Mark Bickerdike, Mojo (left) courtesy of Sharon
Brigden at SLBPR and the Adelphi by the author.

A catalogue record for this book is available from the
British Library.

Typeset in Warnock Pro Semi Bold and Palatino
Printed and bound in the United Kingdom by
Latimer Trend & Company Ltd,
Estover Road, Plymouth, PL6 7PY

Transformation: The Adelphi

Contents

Introduction

THESE are exciting times.

I've been writing about beer and pubs now for almost a quarter of a century and for much of that time it has felt a little like swimming against the tide. Great breweries were being swallowed whole by hungry rivals, fine old pubs were being churned into bland temples of pre-fabricated pleasure, forced to meet the strictures of some ill-fitting brand.

Sometimes it was pitiful to see. It was as if the lovely walnut dashboard of a veteran Bentley had been replaced with glossy plastic trim and the paintwork slapped up with go-faster stripes.

The time was that a pub could open on one of our city's main drinking thoroughfares without any serious consideration to real ale. Perhaps they had a lone Tetley pump tucked away at the end of the bar, but it was incidental to their prime mission of attracting customers in the greatest volume while expending the least possible effort in the cellars. These punters had no expectation of anything more interesting than mass-produced keg ale and lager; the pubs did nothing to raise these expectations.

Those dark days are long gone. New breweries open every week, new beers arrive in our bars daily, whether traditional cask ales or newer craft beers in keg, bottle and can, opening to the drinker a variety of taste experiences unimaginable just ten years ago.

Wonderful world: The Burger Bar at the revitalised Belgrave

Our better pubs have also introduced us to the fabulous world of beer from beyond these shores – astonishing craft beers from America, wheat beers from Germany, traditional lagers from the Czech Republic, and the jaw-dropping range of styles and flavours which have been created over many centuries in Belgium.

Breweries in Italy, Spain, Brazil, Australia – actually just about everywhere – are changing our perception of beers from around the world.

Through the brewers' art, through their delicate, nuanced use of different yeast strains and varieties of hop and malt, the beers produced can vary massively in strength, texture and colour, while offering a whole range of flavours from sharp and citric to chocolatey, treacly and burnt, from sweet to sour, by way of biscuit, passion fruit, nuts, earthiness, whisky – and a whole lot more besides.

Now it's hard to imagine new premises which fail to cater for the burgeoning demand. And if I had to choose a single bar to typify this wonderful new world, it would be The Belgrave,

The Great Leeds Pub Crawl

All our yesterdays: Tetley horses at the Garden Gate in Hunslet

where a cavernous warehouse has been brought back to life with a business based around great beer, lively atmosphere and interesting food. The Black Swan is another that offers a model for how it might be done.

Perhaps there was a tipping point, a moment that sparked this transformational change. If there was, I missed it, but either by stages or by stealth this wonderful new age has emerged.

The 63 pubs and bars on my *Great Leeds Pub Crawl* are some of my personal favourites and between them represent a broad cross-section of the licensed premises to be found in my home town. There are seven crawls, each of nine pubs, but aside from these, I have suggested many others around the city which are also worthy of your custom. Even so, it's not a comprehensive list, and doubtless some readers will feel aggrieved that their own favourites didn't make the cut.

The ones which did each have something special to justify their inclusion, while my suggestion of some detours and some alternative pub crawls in Chapel Allerton, Otley, Wetherby, along Great George Street and Call Lane – plus the infamous Otley Run – should hopefully satisfy even the thirstiest reader.

Simon Jenkins,
25 July 2015

x

Heritage
Route

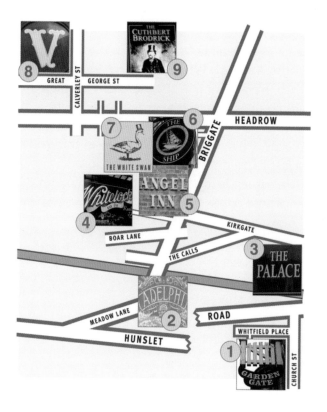

The Great Leeds Pub Crawl

THIS first pub crawl visits some of the best preserved historic pubs in a city which hasn't always afforded them the protection they deserve.

It is comfortably the longest trail described in this book and could be cut in half by simply ignoring the first pub and starting at the Adelphi. Yet to do so would be to leave out the city's finest pub and its licensed premises most deserving of heritage status.

So, visit the **Garden Gate**, and if you can't face the long walk along cheerless Hunslet Road, take a bus or a taxi before completing this little jaunt through some of the city's most unspoiled and historic pubs. It takes in three obvious heritage choices – the **Adelphi**, **Whitelock's** and **Victoria** – though the others each have genuine historic merit of their own. The **Palace** sits on one of the city's earliest settlements; in the **Ship**, **Angel** and **White Swan** can be glimpsed the geometry of ancient Leeds, where homes and businesses thrived cheek-by-jowl in a fast-expanding city.

And it ends at the thoroughly modern **Cuthbert Brodrick**, whose name celebrates the architect responsible for some of Leeds's most iconic buildings.

The Garden Gate

Whitfield Place, Hunslet, LS10 2QB.
☎ 0113 277 7705
www.gardengateleeds.co.uk

OUR journey starts a mile out of town, where, in an unfashionable suburb and surrounded by low-rise offices and seventies housing, lies Leeds's most beautiful pub.

If the Garden Gate were in a fashionable suburb – or close enough to the city centre to be part of the regular crawl – it would be lauded like Whitelock's and the Adelphi and prized

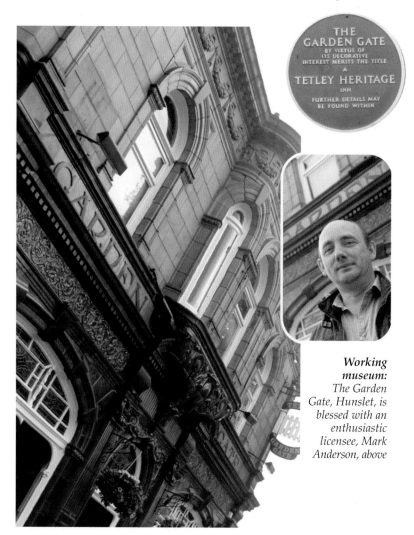

Working museum: *The Garden Gate, Hunslet, is blessed with an enthusiastic licensee, Mark Anderson, above*

yet more highly. Tourists would flock to this working museum and try a pint of traditional hand-pulled ale, Nikons clicking like grasshoppers.

But the Garden Gate hangs at the end of a characterless cul-de-sac in downtown Hunslet, lost in its surroundings.

It has served this community since before Queen Victoria's

reign. Abandoned changing rooms in the cellar speak of a time when it doubled as home to the local rugby league side. The showers, the communal bath, the masseur's table, are all still there, relics of a glorious past when every pub, factory and church fielded teams to carry their proud names across the whitewash. One can imagine great hulks of working men, stirred to the cause and striding into battle, local honour at stake.

Ghosts must hang here, echoes of these great warriors, stepping through the fine hot mist of the showers, nursing their wounds and cursing still.

They might find today's society bewildering, fractured and lost, but drifting upstairs for an after-match pint, they would recognise much about the Garden Gate.

It is a ceramic palace, from the ornate brown and cream tiled exterior, to the greens of the pub's long central corridor which divides little snugs, nooks and crannies from the two main drinking areas either side of a central bar.

The corridor is itself a gem, tiled from floor to ceiling, save for polished mahogany panels and panes of etched and decorated glass. The floor is an ornate tiled mosaic; a tiled archway arcs over the corridor. Wood, mirrors and glass predominate in each room, though it's the ceramic which makes this place truly special. It's only a part-romantic notion that these tiles are Burmantofts Faïence, a relic of the time when the east Leeds suburb was famed for its pottery. The present building – a perfect example of late Victorian and early Edwardian architecture – dates from 1902, when pottery production at Burmantofts was still in full swing.

The curving bar counter, tiled floors and mahogany back bar of the Garden Gate's front room, the Vaults, is an absolute treasure, and alone worth the pub's elevation to Grade II* listed status.

Londoner Mark Anderson is working hard to reconnect the Garden Gate with its local community and particularly with its rugby side. Hunslet Hawks memorabilia dominates the decor. "I walked in and fell in love with the place," he tells me.

Listed:
The Garden Gate

Pub architecture

BETWEEN the mahogany panelling of the **Adelphi**, the spectacular ceramic of the **Garden Gate** and the exuberant gaudy mirrors, stained glass, dark wood, brass and copper bar-top of **Whitelock's**, Leeds boasts some true gems of pub internal architecture. Others have merit, the curious mock Tudor of the **Templar**, the Victorian utility of the **Cardigan Arms** and the faded grandeur of the **Duck & Drake**.

Given the constant throughput of customers and regular changes of ownership and direction they have endured, it is perhaps remarkable they have survived intact.

As at the Garden Gate there are some further gems to be found in the

suburbs: Headingley's **Original Oak** and Chapel Allerton's stately **Mustard Pot** have retained some of their original charms, though many others like the **Queens** in Harrogate Road and **Brownlee Arms** in Horsforth have, in successive refurbishments, been stripped of their character in the name of progress.

Worse still, some fine old pubs stand boarded up or unloved.

The **Beech**, an art deco period piece in Wortley, the cosy **Albion** in Armley, famous as the model used for a 00-scale trackside pub in the old Hornby Railway, and the ornate **Rising Sun** in Kirkstall, haven't served a pint in years ●

The Great Leeds Pub Crawl

▎ The Adelphi Hotel

Hunslet Road, LS10 1JQ.
☎ **0113 245 6377**
www.theadelphileeds.co.uk

JUST a few yards from the Tetley gates, the beautiful Adelphi was the de facto brewery tap for more than one hundred years. Staff would slake their thirst after long days in the brewhouse, bottling plant, warehouses and delivery vans.

Its frontage is a shapely, stately, elegant curve; stepping inside is to get a glimpse of the creative workmanship essential to a Victorian city tavern. Its levels of comfort would be far greater than those enjoyed by many of its customers at home.

Like the Garden Gate, Whitelock's and Victoria – all stopping points on this first pub crawl – the Adelphi is a true pub gem, its heavy doors framed with extravagant carved wooden surrounds, windows of floral etched glass, acres of lacquered wood and red tiles. Some of the seating is still separated by wood and glass screens which act as an effective baffle to conversation, while the pub's separate high-ceilinged rooms each has its own character and ambience. The sumptuous colours of the tasteful redecoration lend a contemporary feel.

The bar, which stretches along the pub's central corridor,

Tetley Brewery

THE walk from The Garden Gate to the Adelphi takes 20 minutes and brings you directly past the sprawling site of Tetley brewery, which closed in June 2010.

Its bright red letters shone through clouds of billowing steam for generations, as sure a "Welcome to Leeds" for travellers arriving from the south as the ivory white of the Parkinson Tower, the stone grandeur of the Town Hall or the bronze bulk of the Black Prince statue.

*A **glittering gem:** The Adelphi offers a sumptuous drinking environment*

fronts onto just two of these rooms and is topped with an ever-changing range of ales and a cosmopolitan choice of lagers.

With its days as the Tetley brewery tap long gone, the Adelphi has re-invented itself as a gastropub, serving the chef's high-end take on some familiar pub grub choices.

Upstairs, a large function room is in big demand for parties and events; an enclosed courtyard offers outdoor drinking and dining.

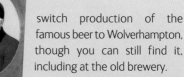

The beer itself was as much a part of the city as Roundhay Park, the City Varieties, the all-white strip; the hunstman logo was utterly synonymous with Leeds.

Owners Carlsberg may have underestimated drinkers' passion for a local product when they decided to switch production of the famous beer to Wolverhampton, though you can still find it, including at the old brewery.

Nowadays it is re-invented as The Tetley, a lively centre for the arts, events, dining and – oh, the irony – real ale.

www.thetetley.org

The Palace

Kirkgate, LS2 7DJ.
☎ **0113 244 5882**
www.nicholsonspubs.co.uk

TO visit Kirkgate is to journey into the earliest parts of our city. There has been a church here since at least the 11th century; the current Minster – formerly Leeds Parish Church – was consecrated in 1841.

The Palace opened at around the same time, but the building itself dates back at least another century, when it was the grand home of timber merchant Edmund Maude.

The arrival of the Leeds-Liverpool canal and Aire and Calder Navigation made this part of the city a thriving hive of commercial activity – and one Palace landlord even built boats behind the pub.

The slow post-war decline of the area might have been

Historic site: The Palace sits in one of the oldest parts of the city

terminal, but for the invention of 'city living' and the rapid gentrification of this area of neglect. The arrival of new flats, businesses and hotels have created for this great old pub a fresh constituency.

It is every bit the classic alehouse, a U-shaped arrangement of rooms clustered around a central bar topped with handpulls serving up to ten real ales. A CAMRA award at the end of 2014 not only acknowledged this commitment to great beer, but was also a personal accolade for long-serving licensee Terry Grayson, who has now retired after more than 15 years here.

Hooded globe lanterns hang over the main bar which dog-legs into a drinking space to the right of the main door. The furniture is by turns leather sofas and wooden-topped stools, the decor burgundy, chocolate and white, and the main bar area is dominated by a brick fireplace and a great old

Early History

SOME of the key moments in the city's history are illustrated on a signboard just outside the Palace. When it was first built, the building stood outside the city boundary, whose eastern limits were marked by the East Bar Stone, which can still be seen set into the Minster wall.

The earliest references to the city are in the eighth century writings of Bede who refers to Loidis, though revered 18th century historian Ralph Thoresby asserts the town had Roman origins.

After the conquest – once William had laid waste to the north – the area was bestowed on Norman baron Ilbert de Laci, and as well as Ledes being mentioned in the *Domesday Book* of 1086, nearby settlements such as Ermelei (Armley) and Hedingleia (Headingley) were already established.

An Elizabethan map of the town shows a layout of early streets – Kirkgate, Lowerhead Row, Briggate and Vicar Lane – whose geometry remains largely unchanged today ●

clock atop a column. Out back is an attractive courtyard area, lit by a hundreds of tiny bulbs strung above it like a blanket of stars.

At the front, a paved area affords yet more outdoor drinking space, decorated with attractive hanging baskets. For traffic arriving in the city over Crown Point Bridge, the whitewashed Palace with its green and gold livery and colourful floral displays, must be a very welcome sight. Hearty meals are served every session.

Whitelock's

Turk's Head Yard, LS1 6HB.
☎ 0113 245 3950
www.whitelocksleeds.com

LEEDS's most famous pub is back on the up.

It has endured a chequered recent history amid a sequence of bewildering changes of ownership, management and direction.

But a rescue headed by Ed Mason, owner of Hackney craft brewer Five Points, has seen turnover trebled and a return to the high quality of food and drink which established Whitelocks as a favourite across three centuries of city life. Mason became familiar with the pub during his time as a student; he took over in time to celebrate its 300th anniversary in 2015.

Yet as the splendidly subtitled 'First City Luncheon Bar' it remains recognisably the same lively, welcoming hostelry

A local legend:
Whitelock's

which John Betjeman described as "the very heart of Leeds", as much a home to shoppers, office staff, pensioners and loving couples as it is to visitors, wandering theatricals and passing poets.

Originally the Turk's Head, the pub was run by successive generations of the Whitelock family from the middle of the 19th century, until 1944, when it came under the ownership of Youngers Brewery. The yard itself – a handy shortcut from Land's Lane to Briggate – retains this old name, which echoes with mystery, history and the resonance of the Crusades.

Despite being the city's best-known watering hole, Whitelock's has rarely served the city's most famous beer. For many years Scottish and Newcastle products dominated on the bar and I don't think I've ever found Tetley's here. Youngers Ales

Very heart of Leeds:
Whitelock's has
proved popular with
drinkers, shoppers,
visitors, office staff,
pensioners and poets

are now long gone, replaced by a changing choice of real ales served across the high, broad, copper-topped bar.

Amid the stained glass, polished brass and glinting mirrors, perhaps Whitelock's most remarkable feature is its beautiful curved bar front of sculptured tiles – the rich browns and creams, vibrant yellows and greens.

Its long outside yard is one of the city centre's great outdoor drinking spaces, and gives a clue to the nineteenth century layout of the city.

In 2006, Sarah Whitelock – a descendant of 1860s licensee John Lupton Whitelock – unveiled the pub's blue plaque for historical importance, the 100th to be awarded by Leeds Civic Trust. Look closely and you'll see that some judicious over-painting has corrected an error on the original.

The Great Leeds Pub Crawl

Leeds's oldest pub

WHITELOCK's is routinely claimed to be the oldest pub in Leeds, though it isn't. By the time its first licence was granted in 1715, trading had already been going on at the nearby **Pack Horse** for at least a century.

The current Whitelock's – *pictured right, in 1966* – was shaped by major alterations in 1886, though much of the exterior is likely to date back to 1784, when it was laid out as a pub, brewhouse and cottages. By contrast, the Pack Horse has been rebuilt and remodelled so many times that all its original character is gone.

Yet both are relative striplings compared to the **Bingley Arms**, a few miles east of the city at Bardsey, where detailed records list all the innkeepers and brewers since Samson Elys was first documented as serving those travelling between Leeds and York in 953 AD.

The Bingley is one of a handful nationwide which claim to be Britain's oldest – a rivalry that even the *Guinness Book of Records* has failed to satisfactorily resolve ●

Golden oldie:
The inn at Bardsey

The Angel Inn

Angel Inn Yard, LS1 6LN.
☎ **0113 245 1428**

IF ever a pub were described as having two personalities, then it would probably be the Angel.

It had been closed as licensed premises for many years when it was re-opened by Samuel Smith's in the 1990s – a watch repairer and a tailoring business had shared the building in the meantime.

If nothing else, Sam's brings two guarantees to a pub – decent real ale and low prices. And, just as at Wetherspoons, this pulls in those eager to drink proper cask beer, and those who will drink anything, just so long as it's cheap.

Which all makes for a very mixed clientele. And if you happen upon Angel Inn yard some afternoons you'll find a pretty lively crowd. Yet the fine dining and genteel atmosphere of the Angel's upstairs lounge pulls in a quite different demographic, customers who come in search of relaxation and quality, food and conversation.

It all works remarkably well, not least because – unlike the Ship and Whitelock's, whose ancient alleyway footprint it shares – the Angel is on three levels.

Inside at ground level, elderly chaps ekeing out their pensions gather at the main bar. The decor is spartan, utilitarian, with its wooden floors and benches.

Split personality: The Angel, off Briggate

Yet up the stairway, past fascinating maps of the tight-knit terraces of Victorian Leeds, it is like a completely different place. Leather armchairs, monochrome streetscapes and tartan carpets lend the feel of a sumptuous gentleman's club. Here, a second bar serves the whole range of Sam Smith's products, while menus on every table emphasise that this is also very much the dining area.

Only in the yard outside and in the toilets of the barrel-vaulted cellars do these two rather different groups of drinkers ever meet.

Samuel Smith's Brewery

OVER 250 years old, Sam Smith's is one of the oldest family-owned breweries in the world and one of the few remaining large independents in the UK. By contrast, nearby John Smith's, which started as the result of a Victorian schism in the Smith family, is now owned by the multinational Heineken.

Sam Smith's trades on tradition, with the Old Brewery water drawn from a well sunk more than 200 years ago, a strain of yeast dating back 100 years, hand-weighed hops and fermentation in slate Yorkshire Squares.

Its 200 or so pubs, mostly in Yorkshire, but some spread around the UK, including several in London, sell only Sam Smith's products, a policy that applies as much to the spirits and the snacks as it does to the beers.

Its determined and occasionally quirky independence can seem almost puritanical. The Samuel Smith's name now rarely appears on the front of its very plain-fronted pubs, often denoted with just a simple inn sign.

Few play music to save on performing rights fees, few have websites, they rarely advertise.

Yet the trade-off for this close control on expenditure is that they can charge rock-bottom prices. And their malty, butterscotchy Old Brewery Pale Ale remains a true Yorkshire classic.

www.samuelsmithsbrewery.co.uk

The Ship Inn

Ship Yard LS1 6LL.
☎ **0113 246 8031**
www.theshipleeds.co.uk

WHILE less distinctively opulent than its illustrious near-neighbour, with its renewed commitment to real ale and quality pub food, the Ship now offers some serious competition for Whitelock's.

Long and narrow: The Ship Inn has plenty of cracking beers on offer

They share architectural features – long, narrow, intimate rooms and sheltered yards that are natural outdoor drinking spaces. And while the Ship to some extent is the obvious poor relation, it still has plenty to offer, including some cracking beers.

29

The Great Leeds Pub Crawl

The Lands Lane end of the alley is topped by an attractive iron sign welcoming you to Ship Yard. From Briggate, a dog-legged blind alley leads to the pub's front door. From here you emerge at the end of a long L-shaped bar topped with a decent choice of ales and lagers.

Screens of brass piping, oak and tiled counters and etched glass create a series of intimate little booths, each topped with white globe lanterns. The floor is by turns wooden and carpeted, though the chequerboard tiles around the bar can be a little disorientating if encountered while drunk.

If you're searching for true character here, look up. The ceiling features diamond panels of wood and is lacquered a rich red-brown, while lamps of different styles and brightness are cleverly deployed to effect an impression of warmth. Ornate carvings above the bar offer a further surprise.

A short flight of stairs leads up to a more intimate square dining room at the rear, with racks of gilt-tooled books above red U-shaped leather-look seating which maximises the use of the space. Big mirrors make this poky area seem far bigger.

Here again it's worth looking upwards. An outsize circle has been sculpted into the ceiling to accommodate a much smaller fan. You could probably fit one of the Titanic's propellers into it.

A fair reflection: The Ship sits in a maze of alleyways

Packed: The Bull & Mouth in days when Briggate's yards had dozens of pubs

Briggate's pubs of old

WHITELOCK's and the Ship are a legacy of the time when alleyways on either side of Briggate hid any number of hotels and alehouses. There were once dozens of these yards, crowded with houses, shops and pubs, parallel ginnels of daily life and commerce linking the nascent city's major routes.

Around 1850 there were more than 30 pubs – places with fascinating names like The Bull & Mouth, the Blackwell Ox, the Saddle, the Leopard – between the Headrow (then Upperhead and Lowerhead Row) and the river. Some will have opened after the Beerhouse Act of 1830, which halved the duty on beer and led to the number of licensed premises in Leeds doubling to 545 in a decade, though some were much older, like the Old George,

A slice of history on display:
Though long gone, the entrance to
Briggate's Bay Horse was once
below this sign, the former
landlord Molineaux's name
preserved forever in the brickwork

name–checked by noted 17th century travellers Sir Walter Calverley and Celia Fiennes.

Most of these pubs are gone now, the alleyways bricked up or built over and their utility sacrificed in the name of progress.

Yet in the topography of the Ship, the Angel, Whitelock's and the Pack Horse can be discerned a little of the city's past ●

The White Swan

Swan Street, LS1 6LG.
☎ **0113 242 0187**
www.whiteswanleeds.co.uk

RHODA Rogers' *Saucy Paris Peep Show, Strike a Nude Note* and *Striptease Special* – posters advertising acts from days gone by, many of an explicit nature, chronicle the long connection between the White Swan and the City Varieties upstairs.

That's a venue where a pre-teen Charlie Chaplin once clog-danced, Harry Houdini performed acts of escapology and, most famously, the BBC's *The Good Old Days* was recorded for three decades.

The show's legendary producer Barney Colehan was briefly namechecked by the pub, which was renamed Barney's at some point in the 1980s, amid a dizzying series of changes in which it was both Bar Pacific and the Blue Bar.

Its seedy nature reflected the down-market fare on stage. But just as the City Varieties

Variety links: *The White Swan has a long-standing connection with showbiz*

was reborn in 2011 after a splendid refurbishment, so has the White Swan reclaimed its place as one of Leeds' best watering holes.

Not much sunshine penetrates the high-walled passage of Swan Street, but a Yorkshire Stone pavement outside is a fine place to enjoy one of the Leeds Brewery beers on a warm afternoon.

Inside, the essential shape of the bar is just as it has been for many years, with a long counter along the back wall. Stools are arranged around pillars and high tables here; to the left is a raised corralled area, to the right a carpeted seating area with a baby grand piano and big glass doors which open directly onto the foyer of the Varieties.

If you ask for your beer in a plastic glass, you can take it right through into the auditorium, a civilised by-product of these two great Leeds institutions continuing to work hand-in-glove.

Leeds Brewery

BIG doesn't always equate to beautiful, but one can hardly blame Leeds Brewery for making a feature of its size.

Bottle labels trumpet the fact this is now Leeds's largest brewer. Once the small fry in a city utterly dominated by Tetley's, it has by a happy accident of timing and nomenclature, become the city's undisputed number one.

Crisp, refreshing Leeds Pale is the flagship ale, and in its sessionable and easy–going nature can be glimpsed the whole philosophy of a brewery happy to be in the mainstream. "We don't do weird and wacky," says co–founder Sam Moss. "Other brewers might want to do a 10% raspberry saison, for example, but we don't and we never will."

> "We tell pubs, if you have Leeds Pale on then it's likely to be your best–selling beer..."

And as more brewers have entered the market, Sam is proud that Leeds has more than held its own, winning new business in the face of increased competition: "We tell pubs, if you have Leeds Pale on then it's likely to be your best selling beer. To do that we have to work very hard on consistency.

"We still have a real focus on being local. It's great that our beers are on sale in Scotland and London, but what really matters to us is being on in

The pride of Leeds: Sam Moss and Venkatesh Iyer of Leeds Brewery display their wares

places like the Adelphi." And by having ringed the city centre with a great chain of its own pubs – the White Swan, Midnight Bell (p68), "Lamb & Flag" (p104), Crowd of Favours (p105) and Brewery Tap (p142) – Leeds Brewery has the means to showcase all its beers, and by extension, the talents of baby-faced brewer Venkatesh Iyer.

His classic Yorkshire bitter Leeds Best and rich, dark Midnight Bell are now a familiar sight on handpulls across the city, while sessionable Leodis Lager, juicy Monsoon IPA and smoky, chocolatey Gathering Storm stout have extended the range on keg, allowing Leeds Brewery to get into restaurants, hotels and bars which the cask beers would never reach.

While some others have stretched the envelope to create beers of great strength or bewildering bitterness, this brewery's straight-forward easy-going ales can always be relied on to deliver. "Maybe that marks us out as mainstream," says Sam. "But to me that's no bad thing."

www.leedsbrewery.co.uk

Ornate time travel: The Victoria Hotel

The Victoria Hotel

Great George Street, LS1 3DL.
☎ **0113 245 1386**
www.nicholsonspubs.co.uk

TO visit this wonderful old pub is to step into a different age. The magnificent Victoria Family and Commercial Hotel – to give it its full title – was once a sumptuous working hotel with 27 bedrooms on five floors. An underground tunnel connects it to the Town Hall and was used by judges to scurry between the courtroom and their hotel room without having to face reprisals in the street outside.

Modern fire regulations and the lack of a lift are among the reasons why these rooms now lie empty and unused. In a city where characterless multi-storey concrete hotels do brisk business, it's a serious shame that visitors are denied the opportunity to spend the night in a place of such beauty, interest and heritage. Even so, by simply drinking in the Vic one can get a feel for how it was to be a guest here in its heyday.

While walking into most pubs will bring you straight to the bar, here you first enter an ornate hall of swing doors and etched glass, once the hotel's grand lobby.

Its three drinking spaces – lounge bar, Albert's Bar, Bridget's Bar – open off from the main corridor, though only the first of these has an actual bar, a beautiful period piece, with its carved back bar of dark oak and engraved mirrors crowned by distinctive back-lit arches of stained glass. A magnificent gilt

Sunday name: The Victoria Family & Commercial Hotel is a jewel

frame holds a portrait of Queen Victoria; further images of Prince Albert and the Prince of Wales support the royal theme.

Sturdy pillars spiral from the bar top to the ceiling, where moulded golden rosettes contrast with the terracotta paintwork. Thirties-style light fittings hang overhead, their lamps reflecting from every polished surface. Beautiful brass elephants carry the handrail round the bar.

Along one wall, leather-backed booths separated by hinged screens of frosted glass provide intimate places to meet, eat and drink.

Nine handpumps dispense an ever-changing choice of real ales, many from Yorkshire; the Nicholson's menu guarantees sturdy pub meals.

Astonishingly, in the 1970s the Vic could have been wiped off the map had some philistine town planning scheme been given the go-ahead. Like at the Garden Gate, a public outcry saved the building, and in 1989 it was given special recognition by Leeds Civic Trust for its "splendid Victorian features and contribution to city life." That contribution continues daily.

Great George Street

THE Vic stands roughly half-way along Great George Street, which offers something of a pub crawl itself. At its western end is **The George**, a simple traditional alehouse that is a favourite with those visiting either the Magistrates Courts or Leeds General Infirmary.

From here it's on to the more up-market **Veritas** (see page 153), which combines its role as a real ale gastropub with a working delicatessen.

Then there's the **Victoria**, before you reach the Irish themed **O'Neill's** – and then the underground **Carpe Diem**, an occasional bolthole of mine when I want to watch the cricket in peace.

Edgy cocktail bar **314 In Progress** is next, followed by the appallingly-named **Nation of Shopkeepers** which has recently installed some real ale handpumps. **Epernay** is all about the champagne, obviously, while **Revolution** attracts an exuberant following ●

Royal grandeur:
The Victoria Hotel is
a fine old building

The Great Leeds Pub Crawl

| The Cuthbert Brodrick

Portland Crescent, LS1 3HJ.
☎ **0113 204 8570**
www.jdwetherspoon.co.uk

THOUGH the fabric of the 21st century Cuthbert Brodrick on Millennium Square may not chime with the heritage theme of this pub crawl, its name references the architect who did more than anyone to set the tone and character of Victorian Leeds.

Born in 1831, Cuthbert Brodrick hailed from a well-off family in Hull. After serving a long architecture apprenticeship and soaking up continental influences during the 'grand tour' of classical Europe, he opened his own practice back in his home town.

And there he might have stayed, had he listened to his old mum, who tried to dissuade her son from entering the contest to design Leeds Town Hall, saying he had no chance of success. He ignored her – and designed his own place in the history of Leeds.

Brodrick's grandiose Town Hall, completed in 1858, is a statement of pride, of wealth, of power from a community made newly prosperous through textiles. Its tall columns, broad steps and elegant dome ooze the confidence of the Victorian age. That the Queen should come herself to perform the opening ceremony was surely the clearest sign that Leeds had finally 'arrived'.

Brodrick's contribution to the city skyline did not end there, its grandeur enshrined in his later works such as the Corn Exchange and Mechanics Institute.

The latter, for many years the Civic Theatre, is now the city's museum – and the closest of Brodrick's great buildings to the pub that now bears his name.

It's a Wetherspoons house, where six handpumps offer a

A ray of sunshine: The south-facing terrace of The Cuthbert Brodrick

refreshing alternative to the lager-dominated culture across the square – and at a fraction of the price.

The pub's broad south-facing terrace is essentially in sunshine from dawn until dusk, well on clear days anyhow, offering a perfect vantage point across Millennium Square, where a compendium of city architecture surrounds the people's piazza.

Brodrick's Mechanics Institute is the oldest, and faces the late-Victorian Electric Press, now rediscovered for late-night drinking and eclectic dining. Then there's the 21st century Carriageworks Theatre, the art deco Brotherton Wing, and the Portland Stone splendour of the Civic Hall, as much an icon of the city's 20th century prosperity as the Town Hall was a century earlier.

Over the bar, a sweep of curving frieze reflects this panorama, with huge monochrome images of Millennium Square, collaged and flicker-booked like some Hockney homage to this modern enclosure where the city's present stands shoulder-to-shoulder with its past.

The Great Leeds Pub Crawl

Detours

THIS long walk offers plenty of diversions along the route, even if the characterful **Mulberry** on Hunslet Road, which would have provided a resting place between the Garden Gate and the Adelphi, is now closed.

Between the Adelphi, the Palace and Whitelock's, the route criss-crosses that of the Exchange Quarter (see pages 81–112) though the **Duck & Drake** (p100) is the only one with genuine heritage credentials. You might also call in at the waterside **Oracle** in the former home of the Tetley Brewery Wharf museum.

Further on, the **General Eliott** is an interesting if rather down-at-heel city centre boozer, somewhat in the shadow of its Samuel Smith stablemate, the Angel (p25).

The ancient **Pack Horse** on Briggate can be accommodated without seriously deviating from your route.

A short detour after the White Swan would bring you to the **Horse & Trumpet** on the Headrow, once the proud bearer of Tetley Heritage Pub status.

The trek between there and the Victoria could also take in the **Headrow** pub, once the lovely old Guildford, and the **New Conservatory** in Albion Place, a cavernous underground venue large enough to offer both full-on entertainment and intimate dining from their excellent menu ●

Headrow heritage:
The Horse & Trumpet

42

The Cradle
of Industry

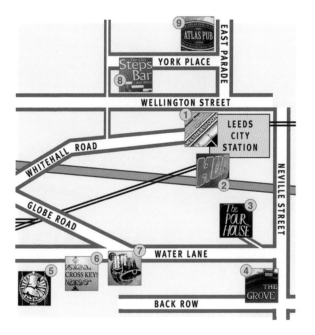

South of the River:
The Midnight Bell

HOLBECK was the birthplace of Leeds as an industrial powerhouse. It became in the late 18th century a hotbed of innovation, gaining for Leeds new wealth as a centre of cutting-edge engineering.

Its confluence of waterways was as pivotal to the city's 18th century expansion as were the railways of the 19th century and the motorways that came along 100 years after that.

This circular pub crawl celebrates a little of that, starting at **Wetherspoons** in the railway station before visiting the **Hop**, set amid the red brick cathedral of the Dark Arches and the waterside **Pour House**. Between the lovely old **Grove** and much newer **Northern Monk**, we pass some of the splendid architecture that remains a legacy of Holbeck's industrial past. Many of these old buildings are being revived for modern use as this once grimy and neglected suburb is rediscovered for 21st century life.

After the **Midnight Bell** and **Cross Keys**, which once slaked the thirst of those who laboured in the foundries and mills, a short walk takes us north of the river and across Wellington Street, once a major hub of the railways, to sample the **Old Steps** and the **Atlas**.

The Great Leeds Pub Crawl

No-nonsense choice: JD Wetherspoons at Leeds City Station

Wetherspoons

THOUGH the Wetherspoon chain is sometimes derided for its cheerful, cut-price, drinking den culture, it has done plenty to ensure drinkers have ready access to proper beer.

Established in an era when cask ale was actually in decline, the company deserves recognition for championing traditional British beer when most chains were heading in the opposite direction.

Morley's **Picture House**, Pudsey's **Crossed Shuttle**, Yeadon's **Clothiers Arms**, Chapel Allerton's **Three Hulats** and Bramley's **Old Unicorn** bring the well-tried Wetherspoon formula to the suburbs,

while the city centre now has several, including the **Stick or Twist** in Merrion Way. Here, a nicely-timed refit has allowed the pub to take full advantage of its position just outside Leeds Arena, which opened in 2013.

Beckett's Bank on Park Row offers a splendid vantage point to watch the world go by. On one side, viewed through giant windows, Park Row bustles with shoppers and traffic. On the other, the ground floor bar is busy with a relentless footfall of customers and the hubbub of conversation.

On Woodhouse Lane is the **Hedley Verity**, named in honour of

▎J D Wetherspoon

Leeds City Station, LS1 4DT.
☎ **0113 247 1676**
www.jdwetherspoon.co.uk

OUR walk around the city's industrial and commercial past begins in premises much more recent. The JD Wetherspoon on the railway station opened in 2002, amid a significant refurbishment of its northern concourse.

It's now over 200 years since the railways arrived in Leeds, the first being a goods line to transport coal from Middleton Colliery into the city. Passenger services began in 1834 with a daily service from Marsh Lane to Selby, and within two decades the new Central Station in Wellington Street was connecting the city with all parts. Leeds Central finally closed in 1967, though

Unfair criticism:
Wetherspoons are
about proper beer

the legendary Yorkshire cricketer, whose heroism on the field preceded true valour in battle. He was mortally wounded leading his company in the Allied invasion of Sicily in July 1943.
www.jdwetherspoon.co.uk

in the dark stone truck lifting tower, Holbeck's abandoned viaducts, the name of a Wellington Street pub – and in the hit single 'Looking for Linda' – its traces remain.

City Station opened in 1938 and is now Britain's second busiest outside London. The planned arrival of HS2 in 2033 will see a further dimension to the city's evolving relationship with rail.

Similarly, the keenly-priced real ale on offer at JD Wetherspoon has added a fresh option for those waiting for a train. A suntrap beer garden is popular with Leeds United fans on matchdays and anyone else in summer; its keenly-priced beer and all-day fare make this a simple, no-nonsense choice.

Perhaps there is something curiously liberating about travel which can free us from the usual social mores. In airports and railway stations, bars trade on this by allowing those of us who would rarely touch a drop before lunchtime, to quaff pints with our breakfast, down shots with a mid-morning coffee.

Here, ten real ale handpulls offer beers from the most familiar to the esoteric, while departure boards in this broad curving space help make sure drinkers reach the platform in time.

*Hop to it:
The flagged square*

The Hop

Granary Wharf, LS1 4BR.
☎ **0113 243 9854**
www.thehopleeds.co.uk

WHOEVER chose to clad some of the sweeping groins of the Dark Arches in clean new brickwork should have first stepped inside the Hop to see how these beautiful industrial features could be better preserved.

Built into the sculptured brick of the Victorian water and rail terminus, the Hop is a perfect, tasteful re-use of this ancient space, exemplary of the way a bar in one of the trendiest parts of town can co-exist happily with the past, embrace tradition and feel comfortable in its red brick skin.

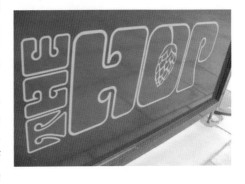

Ossett products are lined up along the bar and further name-checked in sheets of etched glass whose contours follow the high curve of the archways. This was the brewery's first city centre outpost, the nearby Candle Bar is a recent addition to its estate.

Aside from the house beers, there are usually some guest ales also, while blackboards list further keg and bottled choices. I can recommend the pies here too.

The occasional rumble in the brickwork and an accompanying ripple of the pint are a reminder that the arches still fulfil their original purpose, that of connecting Leeds to rail lines running north and east – to York and Hull, Newcastle and Edinburgh. The pub lies underneath the platform.

The Hop's drinking space is enveloped and embraced by the architecture, its gaudy murals of pop and politics entirely at one with the surroundings. Upstairs, where the brickwork fans out like the vaulting of some great gothic abbey, there is a faint echo of the 1960s and the Cavern Club. It's up here that the Hop fulfils its second key function, as a fabulous live music venue.

Pop and politics:
Distinctive decor

The Hop's address is the Dark Arches, yet it also fronts onto a flagged and south-facing sunlit square, with views across to old buildings renascent as homes and restaurants and offices. A redundant lock gate and a dammed stretch of canal are centre-pieces, the once-practical preserved as the aesthetic, and as reminders of the purpose these structures once served.

The Great Leeds Pub Crawl

The Dark Arches

NOW 150 years old, the Dark Arches span the Leeds-Liverpool Canal, and were built as part of an expansion of the railways, high above a right-angled kink in the River Aire. No less an authority than Pevsner's *Architectural Guide* describes this mysterious, mighty brick cavern as "one of the grandest sights of the city today".

The rediscovery of the Dark Arches and Granary Wharf as a centre of business and as a place to live is a model of city regeneration; a fine new use of a space once abandoned, yet now adapted for a much-changed world. Once packed with barges and boats, this was the black heart of the city – smoky, dirty, noisy and teeming with life, beating with its commercial lifeblood: coal and cloth, wool and grain.

To wander through the arches now, to see and hear the rush of the weir, to smell the water and to wonder at this feat of visionary engineering is to glimpse an ambitious Victorian city on the up ●

The Pour House

Canal Wharf, Holbeck.
☎ **07816 481492**
www.thepourhouseleeds.co.uk

THE Pour House is perfectly placed to take advantage of the new popularity of Granary Wharf as a shopping and dining destination. Handily sited between the railway station and the flats and offices of Holbeck, it also has something of the community pub about it too, its Monday quiz nights proving especially popular.

The Pour House opened in 2012, hemmed in by flats and offices on one side and by the canal basin on the other. Just as at its stablemate Atlas (p76), the handpumps dead ahead as you walk in emphasise straight away the company's commitment to real ale. Ilkley's Mary Jane is the regular bitter, while the others offer a rotating selection of guests, primarily from Yorkshire. A

Open flame: The Pour House has learned its lesson

great choice of bottled beers and a selection of quality lagers play well to its knowledgeable clientele.

Inside is warm and intimate drinking, a vision in wood and stone, iron and steel. The decor is drawn from the sombre end of the palette – burgundy, brown and deep blue-black. An open staircase winds to a broad balcony area topped by exposed beams and rafters. Beside the door, a white baby grand is stacked high with board games.

Open fires have been part of the essential make-up of the English public house for generations; fierce warmth, crackling wood and the gentle whiff of smoke lend to the soporific relaxing atmosphere of many a traditional inn.

At the Pour House, they took this a stage further, by setting the roof ablaze – embers from the wood-burning fire catching light in the chimney, forcing an emergency call and a small change of policy. The open fire remains, though thankfully it's now fuelled by safer ethanol.

Housed in the old granary building, the Pour House looks out across the water, while a stone flagged beer garden to the side, dominated by the looming ironwork of an old dockside derrick, offers a special outdoor drinking space.

The Great Leeds Pub Crawl

Waterside revival

ONCE seedy and dangerous, shunned and abandoned, the Leeds waterfront has found a new identity as a safe and attractive place to live, work and socialise.

The arrival of the Royal Armouries in 1996 was the catalyst for major developments along both sides of the river, and remains a significant tourist attraction.

It has been joined by bars, restaurants, offices, student accommodation and high-rise apartment blocks, in a rush to the waterside that has been echoed in many other British cities.

In Leeds, building has been so rapid and space at such a premium, that there is now an almost continuous string of both residential and commercial schemes along the whole length of the River Aire from Wellington Road in the west to South Accommodation Road in the east.

Licensed premises with a direct waterside aspect like the Pour House and aire bar, share with suburban alehouses like the **Rodley Barge** and **Kirkstall Bridge** (p231) that happy opportunity to attract those inexorably drawn by the lure of drinking beside the water ●

▌The Grove Inn

Back Row, LS11 5PL.
☎ 0113 244 1440
www.thegroveinn.com

THE lovely old Grove provides the most striking image of Holbeck's changing landscape. Built as a community local in Victorian times, this traditional real ale and music pub is surrounded by post-millennium glitz – offices, city living apartments and private car parks. It seems a miracle that the

brick-built Grove survived the concrete invasion without being crushed beneath the sole of boot-shaped Bridgewater Place.

And after a worrying time of change in recent years following the departure of long-serving licensee Rachel Scordos, now under the careful stewardship of Dave Graham, *pictured right*, it seems right back on track.

To step inside is to take a small trip back through time, to a public house oblivious to the change outside, where you can compare the relative merits of mild, bitter or stout while listening to a folk band or a guitar duo or just some drunk bashing out a tune on the piano.

The pub retains its attractive old tiled corridor entrance, a nest of rooms on both sides offering the kind of intimacy immediately lost in open-plan designs.

Posters advertise the rear concert room's busy music programme. A piano and a tiny stage fill one corner of the room; bare floorboards, a big gilded mirror, a turned-wood hatstand and candelabra-style lighting lend the feel of some old west

Changing landscape:
The Grove's escape from
the bulldozers is miraculous

saloon. Here you drink off old sewing tables, whose wrought-iron treadles still rock in lovely satisfying fashion, turning the wheel which would once have driven needle through cloth.

Leeds Folk Club – the longest-running group of its kind in the world – has been meeting here on Friday nights since 1962.

Only one room is served directly by a bar, but as at the Adelphi and the Garden Gate and one or two older pubs, the handpumps also front onto a corridor where hatches offer useful extra counter space. The Grove has always had a great reputation for its beer and the choice of eight real ales here is always good.

Despite the change all around and a confusing new configuration of roads which make it slightly tricky to drive to, the Grove remains as relevant, as fascinating, and as worth visiting as it ever was. Perhaps more so.

Old time's sake: The Grove sits in the shadow of Bridgewater Place

Music pubs

ON 27 October 1989, a little-known band called Nirvana played at the sweaty, dirty, much-loved **Duchess of York** in Vicar Lane. Others destined for international fame – including Oasis, Radiohead, the Manic Street Preachers – all graced the Duchess stage. Local acts like Kaiser Chiefs, The Wedding Present, Chumbawamba and Corinne Bailey Rae all cut their teeth here too.

The **Fforde Grene** on Roundhay Road was another launch pad for some big name bands, and the closure of these two legendary venues was a major blow to the live music scene, which is now concentrated in a clutch of smaller venues.

While some feature occasional or weekly live music, for others it remains a part of the daily diet, like at the **Pack Horse** in Woodhouse Lane (p176) and **Brudenell Social Club** (p221). A handful of city bars do the same, like **Nation of Shopkeepers** in Great George Street and the **Sela Bar** in New Briggate.

Tribute acts can often be found at the **New Roscoe** in Bristol Street, itself a homage to the original Roscoe in Chapeltown Road, demolished to make way for the Sheepscar interchange. The Roscoe's terraced frontage is reconstructed in an almost life-size model beside the New Roscoe stage.

The 2013 opening of the **First Direct Arena** has at last attracted the big names back to the city ●

The Cradle of Industry

Northern Monk Refectory

Marshall Street, LS11 9AB.
☎ **0113 243 6430**
www.northernmonk brewco.com

HAVING opened in the autumn of 2014, Northern Monk Refectory gives a new lease of life to a store that once served John Marshall's flax-spinning mill. Established in 1792, Marshall's employed 2,000 people; just a few years earlier this had been a simple cottage industry.

The latter-day rebirth of Holbeck is almost as spectacular, creating in these historic streets a new place to live, work and relax. The continuing success of the Midnight Bell and Cross Keys offers confidence that newcomer Northern Monk, a storey above ground and perhaps a further 100 metres off the beaten track, could similarly succeed.

The ground floor is home to Northern Monk Brewery and now the Refectory gives them the perfect shop window for their goods. Etched glass gives visitors a view onto the gleaming steel vessels of the brewhouse before they climb the iron staircase to 'The Grub & Grog Shop', a broad room which makes much of its industrial heritage.

"It had been used as offices for some years – so of course they had plastered over everything and put in partition walls and suspended ceilings," says Dan Palmer, who heads the 'grog' side of the operation. Partner James Hurst looks after the grub.

"We wanted to see through all that and to the original

Northern Monk brewery

NORTHERN Monk started life as 'cuckoo' brewers – using the equipment in other breweries to create their beers. It was in 2013 that head brewer Brian Dickson moved into the flax store and his beers are now a welcome sight on bars around the region and at festivals further afield.

Regulars include sessionable True North (3.7%), easy-going pale ale Monacus (4.5%) and full-bodied, uber-hopped New World IPA (6.2%). Their potent (6.7%) black IPA is named Dark Arches, honouring another feature of Holbeck's industrial architecture.

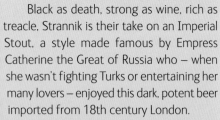

Black as death, strong as wine, rich as treacle, Strannik is their take on an Imperial Stout, a style made famous by Empress Catherine the Great of Russia who – when she wasn't fighting Turks or entertaining her many lovers – enjoyed this dark, potent beer imported from 18th century London.

At 9% ABV, fiercely strong Strannik makes all the right moves – the initial sweetness of treacle giving way to the bitterness of coffee, dark chocolate, woodsmoke and a long throat-soothing aftertaste. Fabulous.

www.northernmonkbrewco.com

American loft-style: Northern Monk is more evidence of Holbeck's rebirth

beauty of the building. So we stripped it right back to the stone floors and the brickwork." Exposed pipework and wires, and the circular hanging lamps which hover over the plain wooden tables lend to the 'American Loft' feel.

Portraits of Marshall and his wife hang in the washroom; a glass cabinet makes an eye-catching museum piece of the building's brass and fabric-hosed fire extinguishers.

The bar is dead ahead, with four handpumps on the counter, and a shiny black back bar studded with 16 taps, predominantly from Northern Monk but with guest cask and keg beers offering further choice.

Food is available all day long – a breakfast menu offers Holbeck's 21st century workforce a healthy start to the day; lunch and dinner menus follow.

THE CROSS KEYS

THE CROSS KEYS

Workers' playtime: The Cross Keys

The Cross Keys

Water Lane, LS11 5WD.
☎ **0113 243 3711**
www.the-crosskeys.com

THE Cross Keys thrived in Holbeck's industrial heyday. Workers drank here; inventor James Watt hired rooms here to spy on rival Matthew Murray, bribing his staff to reveal company secrets. Its pitiful decline matched that of the industry. By the time the North Bar group found it, this historic space was languishing as a tyre store.

A tasteful and comprehensive refit breathed new life into this empty shell, creating a space as fitting for the office workers drawn here by Holbeck's revival as it was for the engineers and foundrymen of Murray's day.

North Bar's only south-of-the-river venue, it stands like a bulwark between the grim edge-of-town car parking of Globe Road and Water Lane, and the glitz, glass and post-Millennium confidence of this resurgent suburb.

With its striking sage green exterior and attractive sunlit courtyard it wouldn't look out of place on the Sussex coast. Step inside and you're transported still further south. There's something curiously French about it, a sort of shabby, careless, messy chic.

Furniture in the main room is arranged around the central bar. Exposed brick and mirrors and a gorgeous long cream sofa create the homely feel of a lived-in yet cared-for place, somewhere which might have been unchanged for centuries. Huge beams criss-cross the ceiling, a spiral staircase is flanked by two red brick fireplaces.

In common with others in the North Bar group, the standard bitter is Prototype. The name suggests it is experimental, soon to be replaced by something permanent, but

Curiously French: The Cross Keys goes in for a 'shabby chic'

it has been a fixture here for years. It's my Friday night ale of choice at Further North and always delivers zingy fruity hoppy bitterness balanced with the soft and easily-refreshing nature of a session ale. It may be a prototype but if they ever change the recipe I'll be the first to complain. The three other handpumps rotate a selection of guest ales, while hearty pub meals are available most sessions.

Special events – beer and food matching, cycle-themed sessions and a popular Sunday evening quiz – keep the punters rolling into a pub steeped in the area's rich industrial heritage.

Bulwark: The spiral staircase is a feature

Ace design:
The interior at
the Cross Keys

North Bar Group

"WE just wanted somewhere ace to drink – at the time Leeds was a bar desert." By creating North Bar as somewhere for themselves to get a decent beer, directors John Gyngell and Christian Townsley became the vanguard of the city's beer revolution.

They expanded via the **Cross Keys**, the small but beautifully formed **Further North** in Chapel Allerton (p228). **Alfred** in Meanwood, **Preston** in Oakwood and **North Bar Social** in Otley are further additions to the chain.

Each – even the tiny bar counter at Further North – serves British ales and a range of authentic quality beers both on draught and in bottle, drawn from every corner of the brewing world.

In May 2015, as they launched their own North Brew beers, John and Christian declared themselves as passionate for the group as ever: "We believe that our bars are living, breathing 'things' and the customers play a massive part in that. It's our staff's passion that makes it work and the customers who breathe life into it." **www.northbar.com**

Preston:
Oakwood

67

The Midnight Bell

Water Lane, LS11 5QN.
☎ **0113 244 5044**
www.midnightbell.co.uk

ABOVE dramatic arches in Foundry Square, the paved patio behind the Midnight Bell, picked out in silver lettering are the words "Welcome to Yorkshire".

It may be the name of the local tourist body, but some 30 miles from the nearest county border, it seems a statement of staggering confidence, as though you have never really reached the White Rose county until you've first set foot in Holbeck.

A few years ago, this is the last place you would have come.

The rediscovery of this once-forsaken place as somewhere to live and work and do business is one of the signal success stories of Leeds over the past two decades. The attractive red brick Midnight Bell is as potent a symbol of this resurgence as the law firms, media groups and e-businesses that have flourished in a suburb which once tapped out the industrial heartbeat of Leeds.

The pub's name gives a clue to its ownership, Midnight

Yorkshire pride:
The Midnight Bell

Bell being the slightly sweet, rich, dark ale brewed by Leeds Brewery. This was their first pub, opened in 2008, and stands where once were the offices of Matthew Murray's foundry. Cast iron plaques in the square – designed to rust and blend with the brickwork – tell his story.

Leeds products dominate on the bar of a pub which has been attractively and sensitively refurbished, rather in the style

69

of a posh Lake District barn conversion. To the left of the door is an intimate, more subtly-lit area than the brighter, slightly livelier spaces around the bar. A staircase from beside the front door leads up to a dining room which is dominated by a brick fireplace topped by a huge stone lintel.

On the landing, plaster has been stripped away to reveal the lovely old red brickwork beneath and the ceiling pulled away to expose gnarled oak beams. The upstairs rooms lend themselves well to receptions, private parties and corporate events.

It's a warm afternoon when I call in; a pint of the crisp and citric Monsoon IPA proves a perfect accompaniment to the sunshine.

Warm welcome: The red brick frontage of the Midnight Bell

History of Holbeck

ECHOES of the city's industrial past are captured anew in the 21st century revival of Holbeck and its re-styling as an 'Urban Village'.

In the 18th and 19th centuries, Holbeck was one of the engine rooms of the world, manufacturing machinery, steam engines and cloth for export across the world, leaving behind a legacy of magnificent buildings.

Landmarks: Thomas Harding's tower works, right, – which once dominated the grim industrial skyline of south Leeds – are being revived for modern use

The Great Leeds Pub Crawl

The splendid Temple Works reflects industrialist John Marshall's fascination with Egypt; the three towers of Thomas Harding's Tower Works honour classical Italian designs – the largest based on Florence's Giotto bell tower. Matthew Murray's Round Foundry, built in 1795, is reputedly the earliest surviving engineering works in the world.

Towards the end of the Victorian era, Holbeck's industrial prominence declined, the Cross Keys's gradual dereliction mirroring that of this whole area. The creative re-discovery of this once-neglected suburb's industrial buildings is a triumph of urban regeneration ●

Back to the future: Just as industrial Holbeck's finest buildings were inspired by Italy, so the modern Candle House apartment block, above, echoes the Leaning Tower of Pisa.

The Old Steps – Bar and Bistro

York Place, LS1 2EY.
☎ 0113 245 0482
www.theoldsteps.com

A STOREY below busy York Place, surrounded by offices, the Old Steps continues to trade well on the accountancy, legal, banking and civil service staff who work close by.

It's small but imperfectly formed: solid tables and comfortable leather chairs make the most of a space which might easily feel awkward, slightly claustrophobic. It's decorated crimson and white with a quarry-tiled floor and punctuated by a sturdy brick column. A clutch of high stools make good use of an alcove area off to one side; the clever use of mirrors effects a little extra space.

The nature of the clientele dictates the hours. Too far off the beaten track to attract passing city-

The jury's in: The Old Steps

Leeds CAMRA Beer Festival

HELD every spring, the Leeds CAMRA Beer, Cider and Perry Festival is one of the biggest in the UK and remains a popular fixture on the city calendar, attracting sizeable crowds to Pudsey Civic Hall.

The event is themed – 2015's festival took on a rugby flavour – with beers chosen from right across the UK to fit the theme, often very loosely.

Some brewers create ales especially–named for the event, or at least rename existing ones to ensure their place on the festival's long bars. Festival–goers vote for the top beer; the award is highly prized by the breweries.

In addition to the panoply of real ales there's always music, good food, and a weird and wonderful

Destination Pudsey:
Leeds CAMRA Beer Festival

Wide choice of
*Real Ales,
Lagers, Ciders
& Soft Drinks*
**Inventive French
& English Cuisine**
*Daily Lunchtime
Specials*

circuit trade, the Old Steps is open until early evening during the week, and not at all at the weekend, save for private functions.

But it's lunchtime when I call in, and it's doing a roaring trade. In the tiny kitchen off to one side, long-serving French chef Raf is working his magic. A steady stream of his keenly-priced lunches are being delivered to besuited and befrocked drinkers all around.

The Old Steps was one of the first bars to serve Leeds Brewery beers and they remain the staple offering here.

choice of ciders and perries, while the global beer bar offers further cosmopolitan choice.

The event doubles as a competitive tasting for CAMRA's prestigious Champion Beer of Britain Awards, where Landlord's Boltmaker and Elland's 1872 have brought the main prize back to Yorkshire in recent years.

www.leeds-camra.com

Strong contender:
*The muscular arched
windows of the Atlas*

The Cradle of Industry

The Atlas Pub

King Street.
☎ **0113 244 2906**
www.atlaspubleeds.com

THERE must have been a temptation to name this the Atlas Bar. A couple of years ago incorporating the word 'pub' into the title might have seemed perverse, but it reflects this city's resurgent love of cask beer perfectly.

Atlas, which opened late in 2013, is ideally placed to exploit the trend. It sits on the corner of King Street and St Paul's Street; close by are offices, banks and the legal heartland of Park Square. On my early evening visit, a group of besuited corporate types file in, thirsty from the mean labours of the day.

The first sight which greets them on arrival at the bar is a line of real ale handpumps dispensing chiefly Yorkshire beers, most brewed in the LS postcodes.

The Great Leeds Pub Crawl

The premises have been tastefully converted, though the layout is much the same as it was in its days as the Create restaurant. Stepping in from the busy junction you emerge into a high-ceilinged, dimly-lit saloon in sober shades of brown and tan. A long central banquette topped by a row of beige-shaded lamps, neatly divides the room's two main drinking areas of dark wooden tables and stained oak flooring.

A crystal chandelier glints above the attractive curves of a chrome spiral staircase which sweeps up towards the more intimate drinking space overhead, the banister twinkling with fairy lights.

The long bar is set into the bold arched windows, allowing daylight to stream through racks of whisky bottles, lending an enticing golden glow to the back bar, and a tempting diversion from the draught products along the polished counter.

The menu covers most of the modern pub dining staples from smoked pastrami to butternut squash, with the accent heavily on fish. I manhandle my way through four inches of crusty white bread stuffed with curried egg and spinach, pausing periodically to dab away stray blobs of spicy sauce from my chin, cheeks, lips, fingers, table and clothing.

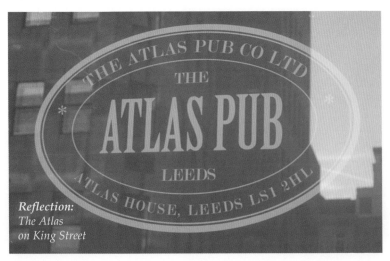

Reflection:
The Atlas
on King Street

Celebrity landlord: Ex-Leeds United star Peter Lorimer owns the Commercial

Detours

THE detours along this circular route are chiefly dining ones – restaurants in Granary Wharf, Holbeck village and around Wellington Street, though after Wetherspoons you might easily drop in on the **White Rose**, just across the station concourse.

It is perhaps no coincidence that the demolition of the Yorkshire Post Newspapers building has hit the licensed trade nearby. The **Central** was boarded up last time I drove past, while the **Wellesley** is long gone. The long and narrow **West Riding**, close enough to City Square to attract a broader clientele, is still there, and always worth a visit.

But newly opened in the circular Candle House is Ossett Brewery's **Candle Bar**, which has brought a great choice of craft ales, wines and Mediterranean food to this landmark location. A visit to the Grove offers the chance deviation to **The Commercial**, a slightly down–at–heel boozer best known for being owned by Leeds United legend Peter Lorimer.

Walking distance: The Queens, above, and Candle Bar are near Leeds Station

You might also fancy dropping in on the **Queens Hotel** bar, whose unprepossessing entrance from City Square suggests little of the gem which lies within.

There may be just one real ale – it was Black Sheep when I last came in – but the chandeliered atmosphere of inter–war decadence compensates for the paucity of choice ●

Exchange
Quarter

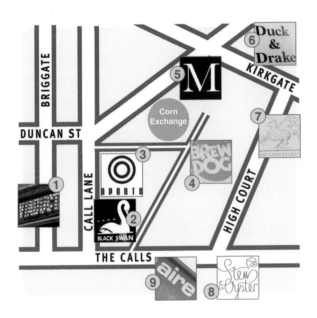

The Great Leeds Pub Crawl

Bright lights: Call Lane Social

CUTHBERT Brodrick's magnificent Victorian Corn Exchange has seen almost constant change in the streetscape over the 150 years since it first opened at the heart of the commercial life of Leeds.

In recent years it has found itself at the centre of a transformation of the city's nightlife, as restaurants and bars have opened in almost every vacant building.

More than any other of the pub crawls in this book, this route has the greatest possibilities for diversions and deviations. If you want Mexican food or Spanish, Italian or French, or if you fancy immersing yourself in the gay scene or discovering the delights of a Pacific tiki bar, if you desire great cask beer or cocktails, or wish to visit some of the bars championing the craft ale revolution, then all those things can be accommodated here.

My route starts in the **Viaduct**, an old Tetley pub re-invented as a gay showbar, and proceeds in a vaguely circular fashion to take in the cask ales of the **Black Swan**, **Duck & Drake** and **Lamb & Flag**, the craft-centric **BrewDog** and **Oporto** and the amazing cocktails of the **Maven**, before ending at the riverside **Stew & Oyster** and **Aire Bar**. Enjoy.

The Viaduct Showbar

Lower Briggate, LS1 6ER.
www.viaductleeds.com

JUST about anything goes at the fabulous Viaduct Showbar, the loud, brash, outrageous heart of the Leeds gay scene.

Years ago the Viaduct was a big Leeds United pub – football flags everywhere, TV sport, Tetley bitter and coach trips to away games. Times have changed, though I suspect some of the punters are the same.

On with the show:
Viaduct Showbar

The Great Leeds Pub Crawl

Even before you step inside you sense something's not quite as it was. Bright lights pick out the words 'Viaduct Showbar', beneath the giant rainbow flag of gay pride. Once inside it's clear that everyone is welcome, whether you are here for the cheap drinks early doors, or looking for a full-on good time under the disco lights and mirrorballs of the dance floor.

There's something happening every night. Monday is Kandyfloss, which means cabaret and cut-priced booze; on Tuesday it's cash karaoke, anyone who sings gets the chance to win a prize. On Wednesdays there are fun games and prizes at Big Mamma's funhouse and on Thursday it's the Pop Tarts disco, with drag DJ Mystique. A big show cabaret act is the major draw on Friday and Saturday nights, while Sunday is a marathon karaoke.

Often camp, sometimes cheesy, always loud, it can get quite hot and sticky in here. The fun spills out into the yard at the side, where trains trundle past on their final approaches to Leeds city station.

It's a gay bar, sure, but it's also a great night out for open-minded folk of any persuasion.

LGBT scene

LEEDS has a vibrant gay nightscene, which is centred around the Calls, Call Lane and Lower Briggate.

Perhaps its best known venue is the **New Penny**, which was founded in 1953 and is the oldest gay bar in the city. Allegedly it's the longest-running gay bar in the UK, and the unknown Lily Savage performed here before stardom came calling.

Close by is the lively **Bridge**, another long-running venue, offering nightly entertainment. **Blayds Bar**, once women-only, is now a popular choice for both sexes, its cobbled yard home to some lively events.

The spacious **Queens Court** combines a large downstairs eating and drinking area, with a comfortable outdoor suntrap and a large nightclub upstairs ●

Black Swan

Call Lane, LS1 7BT.
☎ **0113 827 2349**
www.blackswanleeds.co.uk

FOR all its wonderful bars and restaurants, Call Lane has never properly catered for the real ale drinker.

The flourishing of Jake's Bar and Oporto, Norman and Art's Cafe came before the explosion of interest in British beer, and long before the astonishing growth in craft beers, which has brought such quality and variety to the market. Our thirst for beer was never so evident, the range of ales to quench it never so great.

Even so, Call Lane remains primarily focused on wines, spirits and cocktails, though this shortcoming has been addressed by the Black Swan, which opened in 2015 as one of Leeds's great 'secret' alehouses, quite as deserving of your custom as its more celebrated neighbours.

It's deliberately understated. There's no illuminated sign to show off the name, and it looks every bit an old red brick warehouse or office block. Only the swan motif in the etched glass confirms you're in the right place.

An open secret:
The Black Swan

Stepping inside, you're immediately drawn towards the long bar, fronted with a patchwork of wooden panels, which runs along one wall. Above, behind shelves of colourful spirits, old enamelled signs for beers and breweries, cigarettes and medicines lend the feeling of a backstreet brewhouse, the sort of place you might stumble across in some shady corner of Ghent. It boasts two real ale handpumps as well as a fabulous selection of craft beers – Anchor, Marble and Brooklyn were on display during my weekend visit, with a framboise from our very own Kirkstall Brewery.

Gastronomic delights:
The Black Swan heat is on

Occasional 'tap takeovers' events offer a themed drinking experience, while the pub itself is now contributing some of their own alternatives from their on-site Half Full Beer Company.

This main room is largely open plan, though in the front windows, high-backed leather booths offer genuine intimacy. The room to the right of the front door has some deep comfortable sofas and a small display of cobbler's lasts, for reasons I could only guess at.

Stepping into a room further back, the rustic mismatched furniture and bare careworn brick play to that alehouse feel. There are long benches beside boards of rough-hewn wood and smaller tables, each seemingly reclaimed from some former

purpose. A tired old dartboard, stripped of its numbers and punctured in a thousand places, hangs high on one wall, more for decoration than recreation.

At the end of this room is a copper-fronted pizza oven, whose roaring flames add light, heat and drama in roughly equal measure, while upstairs, the restaurant offers quality gastropub dining.

*Belgian style:
The atmospheric
Black Swan*

The Hourglass

WALKING from the Viaduct and the fleshpots of Lower Briggate to the Black Swan in Call Lane offers the chance of a visit to the Hourglass, a serious real ale and food venue, which began life some years ago as The Hogshead.

I remember the building fondly for its time as the Watson Cairns bicycle store, where I chose a yellow racing bike as my Christmas present, sometime in the mid–70s.

And though the change to the Hourglass has stripped away much of the cycling memorabilia which remained in its Hogshead days, it's well worth checking out the long bar with its fine choice of real ales. Some well–priced pub grub and an intimate upstairs bar are further attractions.

It is part of the Stonegate pub company, which also numbers popular Leeds bars **The Liquorist** in Greek Street and the **Slug and Lettuce** in Park Row among its chain ●

Oporto

Call Lane, LS1 7BT.
☎ **0113 245 4444**
www.oportobar.co.uk

TO me, Oporto has always felt a little as though it were MOJO's southside sibling, a half mile down Briggate, but with the same essential recipe for success.

The big ingredients are terrific music, great booze and fabulous atmosphere. There are differences of emphasis – Oporto offers draught beer, MOJO's cocktail list is more impressive, but they are cut from the same cloth.

From Call Lane you step directly into the slightly shabby main bar, where tall bar stools, plain wooden chairs, and soft low sofas offer a range of seating options. A gap

in the wall leads through to a second drinking space with a stage set up for live bands.

It's all a bold re-use of an old building, and whereas two decades ago everything would have been plastered up and glitzed, here the use of the bare brick and floorboards seems somehow a more sensitive use of this old space, whatever purpose it once served.

There are red lights, red candles, crimson sofas, terracotta plasterwork, and lots of music. From industrial pillars at either end of the room hang

Essential recipe: Oporto on Call Lane

menacing racks of giant black speakers.

Unlike some bars on Call Lane, Oporto serves a decent choice of craft ales, led off by their own Gaslight lager which is made specially by Ilkley Brewery. Northern Monk's Eternal and Leeds Brewery's fabulous Monsoon IPA were further choices on my most recent visit here.

The Great Leeds Pub Crawl

Call Lane

WITH chains of bars along either side of the road offering beer, spirits, cocktails, live music and dance, the lower half of Call Lane is now Hedonism Central in the LS postcodes.

I'm old enough to remember a different Call Lane, one of little shops, bookies and hairdressers. I used to come to the poky Vinyl Tap record shop to flick through their racks of LPs for some interesting nuggets. After dark, prostitutes plied for trade.

Now on Friday and Saturday nights it's perhaps the busiest little quarter of the city. A comprehensive bar crawl here is perhaps best done at a quieter time, when you are less likely to have to waste time queuing to get in or get served.

We could start on the west side of the street at the faintly exclusive **Norman**, recently re-designed with tiled tables, sumptuous leather seating and wooden panels. Twenty–somethings and beautiful people commune beneath a glowing swarm of ornate lanterns.

In the decade from 1945, a craze for tiki bars swept the US, spawned by servicemen who had enjoyed the hospitality of the South Pacific. These proto-theme bars brought thatched walls, carved deities and vibrant fabrics to a society emerging from prohibition and the dark days of depression. Phil and Mel Harrison were similarly inspired by a trip to the Cook Islands – and decided to bring a little bit of tiki to the city too. If it's island indulgence you're after, head upstairs at **Call Lane Social**. Here the bare brick gives way to bamboo walls and puffer fish lanterns, the music is quieter, the atmosphere a little more

Hedonism Central:
Jake's Bar is intriguing

laid back, while the exuberant colours and surfboard-shaped tables play to the Polynesian theme.

Next is that old favourite **Art's Cafe**. There's something faintly NYC about it. With its laid-back cafe ambience and big picture windows onto the busy street, you half expect a yellow cab or crosstown bus to pull up outside. Although there's still draught Moretti on the bar, Art's is now more squarely targeted at the dining trade, with a choice of high-end bar meals served until late every day.

A relative newcomer to the scene, the rather unassuming **Roland** does a surprisingly good choice of draught ales. It's a bar I only discovered as this book went to press – but it's one I want to get to know better soon!

Next is high-octane party venue **Revolution** and the **Brooklyn Bar**, where outdoor drinking space lends an extra dimension to this themed bar with its big burgers and mainstream American beers.

Cross over the road to reach the **Black Swan** (p85), before a visit to the famous Mexican-themed **Neon Cactus** – all tacos and tequila.

After **Oporto** (p88), our little tour ends one storey below street level, in the cool, chic and intriguing **Jake's Bar**, which remains a place that others must measure themselves against, particularly those here in Call Lane. A dog-legged flight of stairs leads down to the cavernous main room, where a line of half-globe lights hang above the brushed steel of the bar top.

Away from this open-plan main room, some more secluded spots in the bowels of the bar offer more intimate and companionable drinking spaces, the white-ceramic brickwork strangely reminiscent of the London underground or some pre-war public toilets ●

The Great Leeds Pub Crawl

▍BrewDog

Crown Street, LS1 7RB.
www.brewdog.com

THEY took their time, but BrewDog finally landed in Leeds in 2013, when White Cloth Court became the tenth destination for the maverick Scottish brewer.

It's a dark, old-brick shrine to craft beer, with its sturdy stone-topped counter and wrought iron spiral of stairs to an upstairs floor with some six-seater booths for sociable drinking.

You'd think the city planners would have welcomed this tasteful and interesting new use of a Victorian building, but – no doubt mindful of the company's penchant for plutonium-strength liquor – they dragged their feet over a decision. "They thought it was going to lead to the downfall of society," says head brewer James Watts. "That's like blaming a Michelin-starred restaurant for obesity."

Courting controversy is right at the heart of the business model. Brewers from Budvar to Black Sheep, Hardknott to Innis

Artful attitude:
Far from bland

Red brick shrine:
BrewDog has a punk ethos

and Gunn are happy to plough their own furrow with the occasional side-swipe at the opposition, but BrewDog have taken it to fresh heights, positioning their rivals as over-fat purveyors of over-hyped, over-priced rubbish, themselves as the clear-sighted white knights of brewing, the defenders of a great craft.

"We have the same attitude to the beer market as the punk bands of the 1970s had towards the music industry – it's a modern rebellion against those beers which are bland, self-satisfied and apathetic," says James.

In a tasting led by James we try deep red, firm-bodied Vagabond Pilsner (4.5% ABV), full of character and perhaps not immediately identifiable as a pilsner; the powerful and blackberry-accented Libertine (7.1%) and the AB Eleven which is actually a 12% barley wine – treacle black and with an almost superfluous extra kick of chipotle peppers. Appropriately, their biggest seller is Punk IPA, where liberal use of Simcoe and Nelson Sauvin hops imparts kiwi and passion fruit, mango and pineapple.

They show some punk-like disrespect to competitors – famously lining up bottles of Heineken for a rather violent game of ten-pin bowling, destroying airborne cans of Tennent's at a clay pigeon shoot, shattering bottles with golf clubs.

As much as I like their beer, and for all that their arrival gives fresh validation to Leeds as a 'beer city', herein lies my

The World's Strongest Beer

BREWDOG's single biggest publicity coup was when they took on German brewer Schorschbräu in a battle to create the world's strongest beer. Tactical Nuclear Penguin (32%) may have been intended as a pre-emptive strike, but became just the first weapon in a cold war of proliferation.

Over-wrought?
BrewDog

ambivalence to BrewDog. That they style themselves as different is fine; to style themselves as unequivocally superior is less easy to stomach. What other brewer would position themselves as the liquid equivalent of high-end dining?

And for all they style products 'beer for punks' and badmouth the big boys, this is a brewery with a serious commercial edge.

A second BrewDog venue, Shuffledog, opened on the corner of New York Street and North Street in the summer of 2015.

BrewDog's Sink The Bismarck (41%) and End of History (55%) – the latter combined with some questionable taxidermy – each responded to the Germans reclaiming this progressive record.

Schorschbock (57%) snatched it back, but now Snake Venom (67.5%), from another Scottish brewer Brewmeister, has set this dangerous bar still higher.

BrewDog has since officially surrendered. After casing your bottles in the furry pelts of eviscerated roadkill there is perhaps nowhere else to go ●

Cocktail hour:
Hot stuff and
English Gardens

The Maven

Call Lane, LS1 7DH.
☎ **0113 243 6047**
www.themavenbar.com

IT's July 23, 2015. You might not be halfway through this book, but the Maven is my very last port of call after many months of assiduous research.

I celebrate with an English Garden cocktail, one of the signature drinks of a bar which the cognoscenti tell me is now the daddy of the Leeds cocktail scene.

Perhaps the reason it took me so long to get here is that it's a 'secret bar' hidden upstairs above a row of shops at the market end of Call Lane. There is no signage outside, just a doorway between an amusement arcade and a piercings shop onto a stairway lined with beautiful ornate tiles – more Burmantofts Faïence maybe – leading up to a bar, where only a large letter M confirms you're in the right place.

"It's the prohibition theme," says bartender Ben Lewis. "Those bars couldn't advertise because it was illegal. We do the same."

With its dark greys and blues, air of discretion and cool, the Maven has the feel of an exclusive gentlemen's club. Comfortable leather sofas in front of giant windows, where net curtains preserve the prohibition privacy. Stuffed owls keep guard over an undulating mountain range of technicolor spirit bottles behind the sturdy panelled bar.

Ben tells me the Maven has won awards for the best cocktails in Yorkshire, is in the top five nationally, and has been named in the top seven secret bars in the country. The last award seems a curious claim to fame – what if some really good prohibition bars had done such a fine job of the secrecy that it prohibited the judges from finding them?

The Great Leeds Pub Crawl

Ben hasn't been here long, but served a valuable apprenticeship during a long mixing career in bars across the north. So while the menu only lists a dozen or so drinks, Ben knows something like 350 recipes by heart. Whatever you order, he can do it.

"It's about passion," he says, while exuberantly preparing my order.

Cocktail culture

HENDRICK's gin, the elderflower spirit St Germain, lemon, cloudy apple juice and sweet gomme syrup are poured over a mound of crushed ice to create the delicately tart and refreshing English Garden, which is extravagantly presented with fresh flowers and a curled shaving of cucumber, *pictured right.* It's one of the most popular drinks at the Maven, and proves a perfect end to a memorable evening out doing the last pieces of research for this guide.

Though the word 'cocktail' has been around for more than 200 years, it was really only in the 1970s and 80s that they became part of mainstream drinking culture in the UK – when places like Leeds's much-missed diners **Damn Yankee** and **Ike's Bistro** began offering their customers an alternative to wine and cold beer.

The colourful swizzle sticks, mini-sparklers and paper parasols are now consigned to the dustbin of history – except for the purposes of post-ironic retro-cool – while dreadful names like Sex On The Beach and Sloe Comfortable Screw have been thankfully abandoned too.

Exclusive cool: *The Maven has the feel of a gentlemen's club*

Instead, cocktails have become a serious business, and plenty of city bars now offer comprehensive lists, competing for prominence by scouring the world for exciting new spirits, introducing ever–more–subtle variations on familiar recipes and demonstrating their delicate magical alchemy with

The Great Leeds Pub Crawl

masterclasses for their customers. At **Call Lane Social**, the cocktails blend south seas rums with tropical fruits and spices.

On a recent visit I tried the Missionaries' Downfall, a colourful take on the mojito, while my wife slurped noisily at the Bula Bula, a rich blend of hazelnut, pineapple and cream served in a halved coconut. Not to be outdone, boss Phil opted for the Amputated Zombie, complete with a flaming liqueur finish, the hallmark of the tiki experience.

Bars like the dimly–lit music-venue **Smokestack**, old favourite **Jake's Bar**, champagne-centric **Epernay**, **Blind Tyger** and **Shear's Yard** will each be somebody's favourite, too.

And for me you can't beat a good Bloody Mary, really sharp, really dirty, really sour ●

No-nonsense alehouse:
Duck & Drake, Kirkgate

The Great Leeds Pub Crawl

▎ Duck & Drake

Kirkgate, LS2 7DR.
☎ **0113 246 5806**
www.duckndrake.co.uk

THE Duck & Drake sits close to a railway bridge in that slightly grimy twilight zone between the Corn Exchange and the back end of the market. The rediscovery of this part of town has seen the arrival of Crowd of Favours and the Outlaws Yacht Club, among others, but has yet to really stretch as far as the Duck.

By comparison to the nearby Palace, its hanging baskets are fallow, its reputation a little intimidating, its exterior less strikingly pretty, its clientele more alternative – and you might easily scurry past.

Yet to do so would be to miss out on one of Leeds's very few unspoiled, no-nonsense city alehouses, with two high-ceilinged, bare-floorboarded rooms serving well-kept real ales in a genuine, lively tavern atmosphere. And at £2.95 a throw, the pub's renowned pie and peas offer good value for reliable sustenance.

The former Scottish and Newcastle pub has long had a reputation for its variety of ales, and an ever-changing blackboard is chalked up with the latest arrivals.

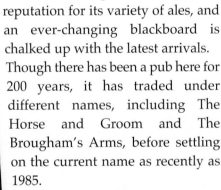

Though there has been a pub here for 200 years, it has traded under different names, including The Horse and Groom and The Brougham's Arms, before settling on the current name as recently as 1985.

The larger of the two rooms is a regular concert venue and across its walls can be found a fascinating collection of vintage posters advertising gigs by the Stones, The Who and T. Rex. A giant mural around the bar features legends like Axl Rose, Stevie Wonder, Elvis, Clapton, Page and Plant.

Beer writer and brewer: Sam Parker

Whippet Brewery

CAMRA stalwart and pub campaigner Sam Parker is the driving force behind the Whippet Brewing Co. established close to Gelderd Road in south Leeds.

It's an area synonymous with the city's sporting history – the Gelderd End is the former name of the Leeds United kop, close by is the site of Fullerton Park speedway, while across Elland Road was the distinctively assymetrical greyhound stadium.

The latter inspired the name of the brewery, and each of Sam's beers continues the canine theme. House Dogge (3.7%) is an easy-drinking bright copper session ale with gentle bitterness and a dry finish. English Whippet (4.8%) is a golden ale with more obvious bitterness than the session ale, yet still with the solid malty backdrop of a Yorkshire ale.

Jet black Little Curre (5.2%) is a rich and complex stout, silky, dark and mysterious beer, with just a suggestion of some smoky dark chocolate and the bitter bite of coffee. Their India Pale Ale Snap Dog (5.7%) is a rich and full bodied ale which features a brace of New Zealand hops, yet the citric nature is not so pronounced as in some American IPAs.

www.whippetbrewing.beer

The Lamb & Flag

Church Row, LS2 7HD.
☎ **0113 243 1255**
www.lambandflagleeds.co.uk

PLENTY of great ideas have begun on the back of a fag packet, but the Lamb & Flag is perhaps the only pub whose name has been inspired by a cigarette card.

It draws on the ecclesiastical. This new red-brick pub is a stone's throw from Leeds Minster and a lamb holding a flag has been a Christian symbol for centuries. But when Leeds Brewery partner Michael Brothwell came across a Churchman's cigarette card with The "Lamb & Flag" symbol (complete with ampersand and speech marks) he chose to adopt it wholesale for this new pub.

The brewery has wrought a fabulous conversion on a

Crowd of Favours

THE late arrival of the Lamb & Flag has bumped the nearby Crowd of Favours out of this pub crawl, though both these Leeds Brewery pubs are certainly worth a visit.

If today's drinking scene is all about charging premium prices for quality beer, served in imaginatively-restored and bizarrely-monikered premises, then Crowd of Favours grasps the spirit of the times and squeezes hard to wrest from it every last drop.

It sits in Harper Street, a characterless backstreet between Kirkgate and the market, just around the corner from the delightful old Duck & Drake. Again the Leeds staples – Pale, Gold, Best and Midnight Bell – lead the way.

The decor here embraces a host of zeitgeist touches – reclaimed furniture, graffiti, interesting artwork, bare brickwork gnarled by the passage of time and a blackboard gin menu.

A metal staircase leads down to a damp cellar sparsely furnished and with a wildly out-of-tune piano for those who like a loose louche feel to their urban drinking.
www.crowdoffavours.co.uk

crumbling 19th century building which was once a signwriter's store and where the lay verger used to have first-floor lodgings. It had stood empty for at least 20 years. Tarting up the paintwork and freeing the bricks from two centuries' grime have made it stand proud of its background at last. You'd be forgiven for thinking it was newly built.

Stepping in from the busy street you enter a stylish, airy, flag-floored bar, whose picture windows and gleaming white walls accentuate the feeling of space. There's a beer garden at the back and a stripped wooden staircase leads up to a more intimate balcony space.

The curving darkwood sideboard of a bar is dead ahead, invitingly crowned with two banks of four real ale handpumps. Naturally Leeds Brewery's flagship products dominate the range, but the selection is augmented by beers from other local brewers.

The menu offers classic pub meals like fish and chips, sirloin steak and a ploughman's lunch (£9.95) – while a specials board allows the chef to stretch out into less well-trodden territory.

Stew & Oyster

Calls Landing, LS2 7EW.
☎ **0113 242 5299**
www.stewandoyster.com

JUST as at Aire Bar next door, a broad terrace affords customers at the Stew & Oyster an unbroken view of the river from Brewery Wharf to Leeds Bridge. Here though it's several feet higher and less prone to flooding.

This was the original, but Stew & Oyster is now a chain with further outlets in Oakwood and Boston Spa, which have

The original: *The Stew & Oyster in Leeds gave birth to others farther afield*

taken the same well-worked formula of interesting pub food, quality beers and a laid-back atmosphere for thirty-somethings and above.

While a tapas restaurant to the front of the premises holds little interest for the serious pub crawler, the Theakston's sign to the side of the building offers genuine promise. The gold letters of Calls Landing, high on one wall of this old red brick warehouse, let you know you are in the right place.

The design makes great use of the surroundings – exposed brick and steel beams celebrate its industrial utility, while some surprising wooden panelling with a carved Chimay motif looks like it was liberated from a Belgian beerhouse. A tiny balcony, with room for just one table, hangs over the water. To one side of the bar, a room opens out into an airy space redolent of a seventies coffee shop, with funky decor and colourful mismatched furniture.

The food, unsurprisingly, majors on stew and oysters,

though their cheese and ham boards and delicious pork pies locate the fare firmly in Yorkshire.

There's a rotating selection of real ales on the bar, plus craft and world beers. Quiz nights and board games bolster its credentials as a community local for the apartments which have sprung up along the north bank of the Aire.

Sunbeam ales

STEW & Oyster was among the first Leeds bars to offer a regular outlet to Leeds's smallest brewery.

Success at a national homebrew contest inspired Nigel Poustie to put Sunbeam on a more commercial footing in 2012.

Initially brewing in his kitchen, his bottled beers were sold exclusively through Far Headingley's superlative Beer Ritz store.

Recently expanded into his garage in LS13, Nigel now produces up to six casks a week which can also be found in bars such as the Brewery Tap, Mr Foley's, The Reliance and the Old Bar.

He is particularly proud of his American-influenced hoppy pale ale Born in LS11 (5.1%), though his floral Honey and Lavender (5.2%) showcases his ability for producing something genuinely innovative.

www.sunbeamales.co.uk

Ray of sunshine:
Nigel Poustie

Unbroken view: The Stew & Oyster has a broad terrace

Aire Bar

The Calls, LS2 7EW.
☎ **0113 245 5500**
www.aire.bar

AS a teenager I remember this part of town as a lonesome place of derelict warehouses, wasteland and dingy, twilight zone businesses clinging to life. After dark you would only visit with sinister intent.

So when this place first opened as Sparrow's Wharf 20 years ago, I'm sure many wondered how it could ever survive. The riverside regeneration was still years from reality; there

Dazzling scene: The Aire Bar

were plans to be approved, buildings to clear, a sceptical public to be convinced.

All has changed. Hotels and bars have revived The Calls; offices and apartments stretch along the south bank; the Aire may not be the Arno, but it shimmers and dazzles, much cleaner than before. Water taxis ply for trade.

For much of this time, Louise Howard has been manager. Originally from the south, she came to join her husband in Leeds: "He was from the north east, so this was half way," and eleven years on, she's still here, one of the longest-serving licensees on the circuit: "I love it here."

Stairs lead down to the main bar, in whose red brick walls and dramatic barrelled ceilings can be discerned its original purpose. These riverside cellars and warehouses once serviced the city's commercial prosperity, when the waterways were the lifeblood of trade with both coasts.

Divided into four distinct spaces, the design makes a virtue of the industrial brick. The floor is part-wooden, part

In love with Leeds:
Manager Louise Howard

smooth slate flags, with leather sofas and stools providing comfortable places to drink.

A long bar stretches along one wall, where shiny fonts offer a good choice of lagers and six handpumps dispense a changing selection of three real ales. Food is served pretty much all day every day, with hearty full English breakfasts from 10am.

Sky Sports helps bring in the punters, but the fact that Louise's neighbouring properties are all residential limits her ability to lay on any high-octane entertainment. Good thing too – Call Lane boasts sufficient late night fleshpots to make Aire Bar a handy bolthole away from that madding crowd. On long summer evenings, the riverside deck really comes into its own; a heated canopy makes it possible to enjoy the changing skyline all year round.

At its highest, the water regularly laps just six inches below the decking, and the bar has been flooded several times during Louise's long tenure. The city's £45m flood alleviation scheme currently under way should prevent it happening again.

The Great Leeds Pub Crawl

Detours

THERE are sufficient bars and pubs of all types scattered around this circuit as to make two or three pub crawls possible.

There's an Ibiza vibe to the **Rock Bar** on Call Lane, and – once you've visited all the bars on that street's busy strip – it's worth exploring some of the others beyond the Corn Exchange.

Before you reach the Maven, there's live music at **Milo**, which sits above noisy nightspot **Wire**. Across the road, hard rock and world beers combine at **Bad Apples**. Around the corner in Kirkgate, the **Regent** seems to be enjoying a resurgence too.

Beyond the Duck & Drake in New York Street is the **Outlaws Yacht Club**, a convert to the craft ale revolution and on route from the Lamb & Flag, you might take a little detour to chilled-out bar restaurant **Shear's Yard** or the more interesting **Wharf Chambers**.

Run as a co-operative this offers affordable space for music, art, film, politics and discussion – and for just £1 membership you can use the bar too ●

Resurgence: *The Regent is one of many Exchange Quarter pubs worth a visit*

Station Circuit

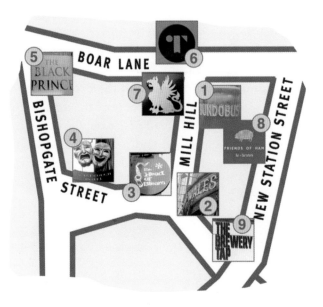

The Great Leeds Pub Crawl

BETWEEN the urgent bustle of Boar Lane and the low thrum of the Dark Arches, something rather wonderful is taking place. Where once the Scarbrough Taps ruled supreme, a whole host of pubs and bars have created the most exciting little pub crawl in the city.

We are living in a golden age of beer – and in few places can the flourishing of this beautiful renaissance be more evident than the spiral of streets just to the north east of Leeds city station. A two-minute walk passes no fewer than nine pubs and bars which have put beer right at the heart of their business.

"It has created an area where people can spend the whole night, rather than having a couple of drinks before moving off," says Claire Kitching, of renowned alco-charcuterie Friends of Ham.

They are so closely packed that you could visit them in any order you choose, but my route takes you from beer-and-curry joint **Bundobust** in Mill Hill to the **Brewery Tap** in New Station Street by way of close neighbours the ancient **Prince of Wales** and thoroughly new **Head of Steam**, the ever-wonderful **Scarbrough**, mainstream food and beer pubs the **Black Prince** and **Griffin**, craft brewhouse **Tapped** and **Friends of Ham**.

A serious hit:
The fare at Bundobust

Bundobust

Mill Hill, LS1 5DQ.
☎ **0113 243 1248**
www.bundobust.com

WE start this circuit at the fabulous craft beer and Indian street food joint which exploded onto the Leeds scene in 2014 and has been a serious hit ever since.

This imaginative combination began life in Bradford as a collaboration between award-winning restaurant Prashad and bier café The Sparrow, ranked in the *Guardian*'s top ten craft beer bars in the UK. After wowing various food and drink pairing events, the two decided to establish a full-time base. A pop-up restaurant at Leeds International Beer Festival gave a taste of great things to come.

The concept is refreshingly simple. Menus on each table list around 15 dishes, some familiar like dhal and bhajis, some less so, like the massala dosa rice crêpes or the vada pav potato

What is Craft Ale?

YOU must have spent the last ten years either in some remote galaxy or in the hardline wing of your local CAMRA branch if you remain unimpressed by the remarkable recent flourishing of craft ale.

Breweries have opened up across the country, new beers have flooded into bars, waves of imports – particularly from the US – have brought new drinking experiences. Traditional styles such as porters, stouts and, most of all, India Pale Ales, have been reinvented. A smörgåsbord of hop varieties have put tastes hitherto unimagined at the disposal of the brewers.

You'd think CAMRA would be pleased, and to be fair, many of their members have embraced this new dimension of modern drinking. But by depriving their beers of the life–giving yeast of a traditional hand–pulled ale, craft brewers have – by its strictest enforcement – placed themselves beyond CAMRA's pale.

It's an accident of history. CAMRA was established to fight the dominant big brewers who had squeezed traditional cask ale to the margins, forcing on their customers pale and characterless keg beers, devoid of flavour and brewed on the cheap.

Forty years on, that battle has been won – wonderful hand–pulled real ales are everywhere, and licensed premises from little arty niche bars to the most cavernous Wetherspoons burgers. Like Spanish tapas, you choose as many as you like to share. Three each should be more than enough.

Further menus list a fabulous array of beers, each chosen to sit perfectly alongside the spicy food. Keg choices like Camden Pale, Saltaire Gold and Schneider Weisse are supported by long lists of beers in can and bottle.

Though Bundobust is a permanent fixture, the particle board tables, the plastic cutlery, paper plates and styrofoam food containers maintain that transient street food feel. The atmosphere is lively, trade is brisk.

thrive on their popularity. Yet CAMRA's definition, which made sense in 1971, now brackets craftsters like BrewDog and Brooklyn with seventies offenders like Whitbread and Watneys.

So what else denotes a craft brewery? Imagination, certainly.

A willingness to experiment and collaborate. An ability to deliver consistent and fresh-tasting beers, whatever the style.

Some would also say it's about size, and that a craft brewer should be small. But who could blame a business for expanding if its products are so good that demand greatly outstrips supply? So long as quality isn't compromised, of course ●

Flourishing scene:
A typically well-stocked bar at the Black Swan

Worth checking out:
The distinctive black front of the Prince of Wales

The Prince of Wales

Mill Hill, LS1 5DQ.
☎ **0113 246 8761**

DESPITE a chequered history that has seen it closed and re-opened several times, the Prince of Wales clings to life. Back in business, this oft-overlooked city centre gem is looking good and doing well.

Always a little in the shadow of the Scarbrough Taps, its short black frontage might be easily missed, or simply bypassed by those familiar with its rather down-beat reputation from ages past. But a refurbishment a few years ago has made this place worth checking out again. There are two handpumps on the bar, and these often serve Leeds Pale or Black Sheep, but not always.

The Great Leeds Pub Crawl

The Prince has the feel of one of those old taverns which you can sometimes stumble across in the backstreets of central London.

The decor is all shades of coffee and cream, with an attractive wood-panelled bar in one corner of the wedge-shaped front room, which has been fitted with a plush black carpet, patterned with foliage.

This motif is echoed in the upholstery of the comfy long banquettes, with their high leather backs.

A quieter, smaller and more intimate room to the rear is a little more basic of decor and furnishing, with bare wooden floors and a pool table.

In both rooms, old black and white prints of city scenes and great old Leeds buildings can be found around the walls.

A small rear yard and a huddle of pavement tables offer some surprising outdoor drinking space, a remarkable suntrap just a stone's throw from the Dark Arches.

Great lost pubs

WHILE every lost pub is mourned by its regulars – great locals like the **Shoulder of Mutton** at Potternewton, **Blooming Rose** in Beeston, the **Skinner's Arms** in Sheepscar, and **Hark to Rover** in West Park – others represent a yet greater loss to the city's heritage.

The late-Victorian **Rising Sun** on Kirkstall Road, with its mosaics and glasswork and curving oak bar, is irreplaceable. It stands boarded up; one can only guess at the damage done to its interior by a recent stint as a low-rent junk shop.

Similarly the **Beech** in Lower Wortley, with its lovely wooden fittings, was looking neglected when I produced the 2011 edition of this book, and it closed shortly afterwards.

Absent friends:
The Beech, left,
and Blooming Rose

The **City of Mabgate** in Burmantofts was once a fine alehouse, steeped in city history.

The majestic **White Stag** in North Street, now demolished, was architecturally a poor man's Garden Gate, and a true Irish pub from the time when Leeds was host to a huge Irish community.

Few though suffered the same fate as the splendid old **Florence Nightingale**, opposite St James's Hospital.

It was destroyed in a gas explosion in April 2008 — much to the chagrin of doctors, nurses and hospital visitors, for whom this was a welcome and appropriately–named bolthole ●

The Head of Steam

Mill Hill, LS1 5DQ.
☎ **0113 243 9070**
www.theheadofsteam.co.uk

THE Head of Steam chain began in Newcastle, spreading to Huddersfield a decade or so ago. Following its takeover by north-east giant Cameron's, the brand is being rolled out to other pubs across their estate close enough to stations to justify the name.

A refurbishment running into six figures replaces tired old Spencers, giving this corner pub with its distinctive curving frontage a fresh lease of life. Yet it is recognisably the same, with a series of intimate drinking and dining spaces clustered around a really beautiful central bar. After years of decline, this lovely old building is finally being treated with the respect it deserves.

A glass and steel sculpture of beer bottles spirals from the bar towards the ceiling, drawing the eye to the narrow balcony which is sadly not broad enough to

Six-figure refurbishment: *The Head of Steam has seven real ale handpumps*

serve as a drinking space, but may play host to live acts in future, like minstrels playing in the gallery.

Those familiar with the HoS at Huddersfield station will recognise the formula – a host of quality beers, decent food and a great atmosphere. But with a strong emphasis on craft beer and a bewildering range of bottles, the Leeds branch, which opened late in 2014, takes this concept to whole new heights with seven real ale handpumps and rows of shiny fonts and all manner of sculpted bartop furniture dispensing cool Americans and interesting Belgians. All the draught beers are available in two-thirds and third-pint measures.

Behind the bar, fridges hold 180 different bottled beers, primarily from Belgium and the US. Drinks menus on each table detail the whole range. The barman suggests a shot glass of something dark and fragrant: "You must try this, it's life-changing." This rich, jet black beer is from the Saugatuck brewery in Michigan; its distinctive, sweet but not cloying combination of vanilla, strawberry and chocolate flavours perfectly combined in the name Neapolitan Milk Stout.

There will always be a Cameron's beer on the bar, and they are contractually obliged to serve Carlsberg too, though why anyone would choose it, amid this wealth of choice, is a mystery.

Railway pub trails

HUDDERSFIELD's Head of Steam is midway through a fabulous ale–by–rail crawl across the Pennines, one of the great rites of passage for the Yorkshire drinker.

Hardcore travellers start with a swift one in **Wetherspoons** or **White Rose** on Leeds station, before boarding the Transpennine Express for a day out at the great pubs close to stations along the line.

First stop is Batley, where the **Cellar Bar** is directly opposite the station. Next is Dewsbury and the excellent **West Riding Refreshment Rooms** in the original station building, then Mirfield and the **Navigation**, which combines a passion for great beer with top–notch food.

In Huddersfield, you are spoiled for choice. The station itself has the **Head of Steam** and **King's Head**, *right*, and, if you venture a little further afield, there's the **Sportsman** nearby and the renowned **Grove** just the other side of the ring road.

Next it's Slaithwaite, which the locals insist on pronouncing Sla'wit. I'm not sure how they pronounce **The Commercial**, but eight real ales should be choice enough, in any dialect. There are ten at the **Riverhead** in Marsden, owned by Ossett Brewery, but with its own microbrewery on site. From here the line meanders dangerously on into Lancashire where the **Railway** at Greenfield and the **Station Buffet** in Stalybridge are options for fearless travellers.

A new guide flags up pubs close to stations on privately–run Keighley and Worth Valley railway, with pubs in Keighley, Crosshills, Oxenhope and Haworth. What's more, the steam trains serve real ale on board too, which is a trick Transpennine Express is missing, so far! ●

The Great Leeds Pub Crawl

The Scarbrough Hotel

Bishopsgate Street, LS1 5DY.
☎ **0113 243 4590**
www.nicholsonspubs.co.uk

DRIVING into Leeds from the M1, the Scarbrough, with its hanging baskets, green and gold tiling and the legend "Ind Coope's Ales", always makes a welcome sight as you emerge from the Dark Arches.

Colourful history:
The Scarbrough Taps

The pub name is often mis-spelled with an additional 'o', but it is named after Henry Scarbrough, the first licensee here in 1826, rather than the Yorkshire resort. It stands on the site of a medieval manor house, Castyll Hall, though the present-day pub is an extension of its 18th century rebuilding.

There are numerous competing theories as to why it's more commonly known as the Scarbrough Taps – or even Scabby Taps – from it once being owned by the waterworks, to tap dancers auditioning here in the time it was owned by impresario Fred Wood. No-one seems sure.

The interior is a large L-shape wrapped around a long bar topped with a great range of real ale handpumps. Where previously the bar bulged out in the middle, cramping the space between the counter and the door, the most recent re-modelling saw this pushed back, affording a good deal of extra space.

I dare say that on Fridays and Saturdays, on matchdays and at Christmas, there will still be the same good-natured squash in here.

Just as at the nearby Prince of Wales, the Scarbrough makes the most of its south-facing pavement to create a narrow outdoor drinking space, a big draw when the sun shines, despite relentless traffic on the inner-city loop.

In long-serving licensee Toby Flint, the Scarbrough has one of the best-known characters of the local pub scene. Toby

Nicholson's

THE Nicholson's chain maintains a level of distinction that sets its pubs apart from those in the rest of the Mitchells and Butlers conglomerate.

It was established by William Nicholson, a Victorian distiller who loaned Lord's cricket ground the money to build their famous pavilion. In gratitude, the iconic 'egg and bacon' stripes of the MCC logo were taken in homage to the colours of Nicholson's gin.

Their pubs are generally interesting, characterful, historic inns, with a good choice of great handpulled ales and quality pub meals. The three in Leeds – the **Scarbrough**, **Palace** (p18) and **Victoria** (p37) are all very much worth a visit.

Cornwall's St Austell brewery brews the excellent Nicholson's Pale Ale, which is the sessionable house beer and a good place to start as you browse the range.

www.nicholsonspubs.co.uk

The right chemistry: Toby Flint is a well-known character in Leeds

was more than two years into his postgraduate research at Leeds University before deciding to concentrate on the pub trade.

After a spell at Whitelock's he was charged with the task of turning round the fortunes of the Scarbrough Hotel. Within two years it was CAMRA's pub of the year; biochemistry's loss was licensing's gain.

The Black Prince

City Square, LS1 1DA.
☎ **0113 245 8063**
www.sizzlingpubs.co.uk

THE Black Prince occupies one of the prized locations in the city centre, on the corner of City Square, midway between the railway station and Trinity Quarter. Built in 1843, this Grade II listed building with its wonderful stone-columned exterior was originally a bank, but most recently was Flares nightclub, where those of us of a certain age would enjoy dancing to the music of the Bee Gees and The Human League. I only went once, honest.

Wonderful features:
The Black Prince

Splendid views: A broad balcony breaks the internal space very effectively

Re-invented as a pub, the Black Prince makes much more of its wonderful original features, notably a broad balcony which stretches above the main drinking space offering views through the tall windows over the square. Its wonderful domed roof is three storeys above the broad, curving, street-level drinking space, tastefully decorated in grey, white and a deep blue-green.

It's here that you enter as you step up beneath a brass lantern and dazzling chandelier from City Square.

The Black Prince goes big on keenly-priced food, offering the same Sizzling Pubs menu which will be familiar to those who have tried the True Briton in Meanwood, Barley Mow in Bramley or Vesper Gate in Kirkstall.

The stock-in-trade is red-hot skillets of chicken, steak and ribs, but the menu covers most of the major bases, with two-for-one deals ensuring that even-numbered parties always get the best of it.

There are six real ales on offer here and the range changes

The Great Leeds Pub Crawl

City Square

THE story of how Edward of Woodstock – who never once came to Leeds and spent most of his life in Oxfordshire and France – came to dominate the heart of the city's most prominent location is an interesting one.

Unveiled in 1903, the equestrian statue of the Black Prince was commissioned by one-time Lord Mayor Colonel Harding, who said the hero of Crécy and Poitiers was "...the flower of English chivalry, the upholder of the liberties of the English people and an emblem of manly and unselfish virtues." No local figure was considered of sufficient importance to occupy this prime site.

Seven years in the making, the vast statue was too large for a British foundry and had to be cast in Belgium, completing its journey by barge from Hull.

The Black Prince is the centrepiece of an array of statues in the square, including local worthies such as John Harrison and Walter Hook. The chap who appears to be holding a table tennis bat is in fact Joseph Priestley, the father of modern chemistry ●

regularly. It's a mark of how times have changed that a mass-market city centre pub now places real ale right at the heart of everything it does. Compare this with the soulless Square On The Lane, which dominated the Saturday night trade in this part of town for a decade, and where you would have struggled to find any proper beer at all.

If you are seeking out niche craft ales, or handpulled beers that you've never tried before, then a couple of others on this circuit would be your first choice, but for good value – in a magnificent old building – you would come here first.

Tapped

Boar Lane, LS1 5EL.
☎ **0113 244 1953**
www.tappedleeds.co.uk

THE Tapped Beer Company, which opened on the side of the Trinity Quarter in 2013, has brought to Leeds the same passion for great beer and hospitality that has both refreshed and educated drinkers at Sheffield Tap, the Euston Tap and Pivní in York in roughly equal measure.

A double set of glass doors offers an effective baffle from the world outside, shutting out the noise and bustle, and opening onto a simple, single-storey bar whose left-hand side is dominated by the dramatic polished steel of the brewhouse; the right side by the bar.

The design makes a virtue of the ugly – a line of chunky steel pipes connecting brewery and bar cross a ceiling scarred

Polished steel: *Tapped is a beautifully designed venue*

131

Virtue of ugliness: There are plenty of pipes but no handpumps in Tapped

by a maze of foil-clad aircon pipes. There's a spirited hubbub of noise.

A long central table offers a raised dining space. Leather-upholstered booths and squat square tables dominate the rest of the space twixt bar and brewhouse.

To the right is a long bar in American cherry wood, where beer choices are bulldog-clipped at ceiling level, so drinkers can browse carefully before making a choice, a bit like at a beer festival.

Even so, it would be easy to assume that Tapped doesn't serve any beer at all. There are no handpumps on the bar, no shiny lager fonts. Instead, all 27 beers are dispensed US-style, from taps set into the copper-fronted stillage behind the bar. Shiny 1,500-litre serving tanks at one end of the bar store the fresh beer brewed in the Czech-built fermenters across the room. A giant oven dispenses colourful steaming pizzas.

Ten years ago this would all have been unthinkable, just seven or eight years ago, this would have been the dreadful Square on the Lane.

Boar Lane

BOAR Lane has long been one of our city's major arteries. Running parallel to the river, it fringed the southern side of the nascent city in medieval times, linking the moated manor house of Castyll Hall to the taverns and workshops of Briggate, always the beating heart of Leeds life.

It has seen the plague and a Civil War skirmish, been a desirable address to the 18th century gentry, and was then laid out again by the city fathers as a centre for commerce as wool underpinned our Victorian prosperity.

In recent years Boar Lane has been tainted by the scourge of urban decay. Those lovely old shops which remained, found themselves cheek-by-jowl with cheap stores and fast food joints. Trouble sometimes flared; this was somewhere you would avoid on Friday nights.

Lovely old Trinity Church has been the one fixture during 300 years of constant change, watching over the fluctuating fortunes of this thoroughfare of trade for generations, its name now adopted by the bold shopping centre which has proved a catalyst for Boar Lane's resurgence ●

The Griffin

Boar Lane, LS1 5DF.
☎ **0113 245 2803**
www.taylor-walker.co.uk

FOR ages this was the soulless Censsa Bar, which stood boarded up and neglected for years, an ugly blight on the face of Boar Lane, until it reopened late in 2014. Its new incarnation reaches

back further into the past, to when this was the gothic revivalist Griffin Hotel.

The new look embraces this history. "Est 1872" is etched into the mirrors behind the bar, while lovely lanterns and sepia photographs of trams and shops invoke the same character. The tasteful refurbishment – deep blues, tiled columns, comfortable banquettes and broad wooden tables – is all in keeping with this heritage. Light floods in through architect Thomas Ambler's stone-arched windows.

Restored to life:
The Griffin

Inside, the pub stretches back and dog-legs around to the right, to reveal the rather surprising 'tunnel room', an intimate drinking space with candlelit tables and period artwork, the barrel-ceiling clad in white tiles like an Edwardian tube station.

The long attractive bar features banks of handpumps dispensing six real ales, two of which are regulars, Fuller's London Pride and 1730 pale ale, the house beer of pub company Taylor Walker, which has wrought this remarkable change at the Griffin. The other four offer a changing selection of guest ales, chiefly drawn from breweries in the Leeds area.

There are further delights of course – not least chrome fonts offering a host of alternatives such as Punk IPA from Scotland's BrewDog, Grimbergen from Belgium and American-influenced Thirteen Guns from Thwaites in Lancashire.

The hotel's Victorian customers might be a little bemused by pulled pork nachos or beetroot and butternut squash burgers, but I'm sure they would recognise the commitment to great fare and warm hospitality restored to this wonderful old building.

Gothic revival: The warmly-hospitable Griffin has gone back to the future

Dining pubs

PUBS have long been a popular fall-back for those looking to eat out, whether for a sturdy, reasonably-priced dinner, or a simple lunchtime refuelling stop.

And while many simply offer the cook-to-formula menus of the big pub chains, Leeds still has plenty of pubs proud to offer seriously good food. The **Reliance**, **Cross Keys**, **Veritas** and **Adelphi** are among city centre dining favourites.

In recent years, the explosion of gastropubs – plus the growing awareness of beer, rather than wine, as an ideal match for food – has extended beyond all measure the range of dining options available to pub-goers, who are increasingly receptive to the idea of pairing different food with specially-selected beers ●

Pub and charcuterie:
Friends of Ham

Friends of Ham

New Station Street, LS1 5DL.
☎ 0113 242 0275
www.friendsofham.com

WHEN it opened in 2011, Friends of Ham mapped a daring intersection between craft ale haven and up-market charcuterie.

Beer-wise, it claimed the same territory successfully explored by the likes of the North Bar group. But food-wise it takes North's simple platters of cold meats and cheese to a whole new level, offering enough cured hams, beefs, and craft cheeses to put the average delicatessen to shame.

Four years on, newly expanded and the *Observer Food Monthly*'s Best Place to Drink in the UK, it is so essential a part of the local scene that it's hard to imagine life here without it.

Owners Claire and Anthony Kitching discovered a deep love of beer while travelling in the US, and American influences are frequently in evidence on their bar. House ale Last of the Summer Swine (6.2%) is a big tasting IPA from Holmfirth's Summer Wine brewery, famed for its strong, experimental, highly-hopped American beers.

The four handpulls and ten kegs change regularly: "We always try to go for beers which other bars don't have," says Claire. "People can come in and try a whole range over their night out. It's about appreciating quality over quantity." Accordingly, all the draught ales are available as third-pints.

The upstairs bar area was always rather cramped, with most drinkers choosing to take their beers into the broad basement, where a long table fashioned from hunks of stripped pine and offcuts of scaffolding dominates the centre of the room, ideal for sociable drinking and dining.

But an expansion into the payday loan store next door has created the same upstairs footprint as below, breathing a fresh

The Great Leeds Pub Crawl

Leeds International Beer Festival

LEEDS CAMRA's beer festival has been a spring fixture on local drinkers' calendars for years. The Leeds International Beer Festival is a relative newcomer, but already a much-loved and thirstily-frequented late summer date.

"The CAMRA event is great, but it only really showcases cask beer," says joint-organiser Tyler Kiley. "We wanted to do the same for keg, bottled and canned beer."

A porter from the US, a gooseberry gueuze from Italy, a red ale from Spain, a lager from Sweden – each finds its place alongside the best of British craft brewing at this wonderfully eclectic event. The first in

continental dynamic into this wonderful space. It boasts more bare wood than a Swedish kitchen – big chunky tables, bare floorboards and farmhouse chairs, while leather sofas offer some lounging options.

A shuffle-table provides some old-school entertainment. Essentially it's a bit like curling, but without the ice, the brushes, the heavy iron weights, the skates or the Scotsmen. And it's a lot smaller. You're getting the picture, clearly.

Eclectic showcase: Leeds International Beer Festival is a cosmopolitan delight

2012 attracted 3,000 people; by 2014 numbers had more than tripled.

It wins the battle of the venues hands down. While the real ale fest is in the rather soulless Pudsey Civic Hall, Tyler's event makes wonderful use of Cuthbert Brodrick's municipal palace – the Town Hall.

"When the sun is streaming in and lighting up the organ pipes, it makes it an amazing place to have a drink," he adds, during preparations for the 2015 event. "A seventies village hall on the edge of town just wasn't going to do it for us."

www.leedsbeer.com

The Great Leeds Pub Crawl

▍The Brewery Tap

New Station Street, LS1 5DL.
☎ 0113 243 4414
www.brewerytapleeds.co.uk

THIS is not only Leeds Brewery's official 'tap', it is also an offshoot of their whole brewing operation. From the upstairs bar, windows reveal the gleaming stainless steel of the pub's own micro-brewing operation which produces low-volume kegged beers under their Station Street Brewery banner.

The Brewery Tap holds a prime location on the approach to Leeds City station and is a welcome watering hole for those arriving in the city or preparing for departure.

Behind its frosted glass frontage is a comfortable drinking space alongside a long central bar which features the familiar selection of Leeds ales, plus a changing choice of appealing alternatives and there is a further drinking and dining space upstairs. On my most recent visit I made my first acquaintance with rich-tasting dark Gathering Storm stout, which is surprisingly light on the palate with a suggestion of chocolate.

There's always a good range of continental beers too, a point underlined by a display of enamelled advertisements for the likes of Vedett, Liefman's and Budvar.

The menu brings a confident quality twist to some familiar pub favourites – the ploughman's lunch pairs the brewery's own Midnight Bell chutney with Harrogate Blue cheese; Leeds Best adds bite to the battered haddock.

Prime location:
The Brewery Tap

The Great Leeds Pub Crawl

Detours

THE nine pubs of the station circuit are tightly packed; even the more inebriated pub crawler could navigate between the entire route in a few minutes.

Those happy to venture a little further afield will find some alternatives close by. Of the two **Yates's** venues in Leeds – the other is in Woodhouse Lane – the Boar Lane branch is the better. Moments away from the Griffin, it combines straightforward pub food, an interesting drinks menu and the kind of anything–goes, lively atmosphere you would expect of the brand. Close to Tapped in the dramatic steel and glass of the Trinity Quarter, a clutch of bars are all worth a visit.

On the ground floor and tucked in behind Trinity Church, **Botanist** offers a funky mix of craft ales, bottled beers and cocktails, while on the second floor the **Alchemist**, more firmly in wine bar territory, makes the most of its elevated position. Mind you, penthouse–level cocktail bar and restaurant **Angelica** trumps them all for views ●

Funky mix: The Botanist can be found behind Leeds Trinity Church

University
Circuit

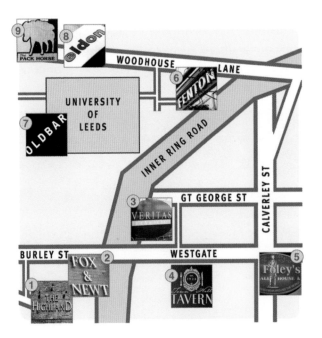

The Great Leeds Pub Crawl

THE sprawling Leeds University campus, just to the north west of the city centre, is fringed with a little ring of pubs which form a decent pub crawl all of their own.

While a few years ago, students might have been satisfied with bog-standard keg beer and cheap lager, now they are in the vanguard of the beer revolution; pubs close to their well-beaten paths are trading high on the popularity of real ale and craft keg. It's probably a coincidence, but beards are right back in, too.

On this route, we begin at the **Highland** and **Fox and Newt**, close to the student accommodation blocks on Burley Road, before visiting three great real ale pubs in the west end of the city centre – **Veritas**, the **Town Hall Tavern** and **Mr Foley's**, and then heading to Woodhouse Lane, where the **Fenton**, **Old Bar** on the University of Leeds campus, **Eldon** and **Pack Horse** provide an alternative education for students of both Leeds and the newly-renamed Leeds Beckett universities.

Beer studies: *The Old Bar at Leeds University*

146

Real curiosity:
The Highland

The Highland

Cavendish Street, LS3 1LY.
☎ **0113 242 8592**

THERE's a faded monochrome advertisement in the lounge to one side of the Highland, encouraging drinkers to try "Tetley Ales with the traditional flavour".

Another archive photograph shows off the famous shire horses pulling a Tetley dray; an *Evening Post* front page from 1923 celebrates the brewer's centenary.

The Highland was once a proud Tetley pub, and though the company's famous huntsman can still be seen on the bar, Leeds Pale and Doom Bar have muscled in on his monocled monopoly.

This great little two-room alehouse is an architectural curiosity, formed from knocking two terraced houses together. Approaching along Cavendish Street you do get a sense of its unlikely geometry, a graceful wedge of red brick which tapers to bay windows just a metre and a half across, like the prow of a ship run aground in the cobbles.

Stepping inside, you enter a well-kept narrow main bar area; to the right is a smaller, squarer snug. The bar itself is a little gem, an elegant free-standing sideboard of curved and panelled mahogany like something you might expect to find on a twenties steamer on the Nile.

There are some nice touches. An old carpet has been lifted to reveal an attractive tiled floor; plaid bar stools and tartan cushions and curtains play to the Highland theme. A dart board and Sky Sports provide entertainment when you're done with the artefacts.

Journalists' pubs

THE curving seats in the window of the Highland were once the preserve of a hardy band of *Evening Post* journalists, who would wander up here for a beer and a lunchtime sandwich, and roll gently back downhill to work an hour or more later.

Two of them eventually bought a bar of their own, the excellent little **Old Steps** (p72) in York Place, so naturally the *YEP* crowd soon drifted away. The closure of the newspaper's Wellington Street premises removed from either pub a lucrative source of trade. The same issue may be blighting the future of the nearby **Central**, which was closed at the time of writing.

Beer and journalism have gone hand in hand for generations.

When the *YEP* was based in Albion Street, **Whitelock's** (p20) was the place where writers would meet contacts to share shady gossip and gain the inside track. John Betjeman likened it to Fleet Street's famous Cheshire Cheese.

Its proximity to the courts made the **Town Hall Tavern** (p158) a favourite hangout for hacks, lawyers and the police. As a young weekly newspaper reporter I was brought here for an eye-opening lunch by a hardened *YEP* journo when we were both covering the same case, sometime in the mid-eighties.

For a while the **Wig and Pen** in Wellington Street chased the same market, but with limited success ●

*Mahogany:
The Highland's
well-kept bar*

Thriving again:
Imogen Bennett at
the Fox & Newt

Fox & Newt

Burley Street, LS3 1LD.
☎ 0113 245 4527
www.burleystreetbrewhouse.co.uk

"I'VE lived in Leeds for years and never known about this place," said one of my colleagues when I first introduced him to the Fox & Newt on an office night out.

It's a pub which has endured numerous ups and downs over the years, and from time to time the brewhouse has been left unloved and out-of-use downstairs, but under the careful stewardship of Imogen Bennett and her team, the Fox seems to be thriving once again.

And just as the tiny brewhouse produces a good choice of ales, the tiny kitchen behind the bar turns out some imaginative food.

This is all pretty appropriate, given that this was once Britain's smallest hotel. The one-bedroom Rutland operated here from Victorian times – you can still see the name in the stonework – until the 1970s, when a gas explosion wrecked the neighbouring shop. When it re-opened as the Fox & Newt, the drinking area had been expanded into the blast site.

The pub's catchment area has changed beyond all recognition. The residential area it once served has seen terraces cleared and the inner ring road slice through its heartland. Though some homes remain and there is a high-rise estate beyond its back door, the Fox's position outside the city's main circuit reduces its potential for casual passing trade.

With its alehouse atmosphere and no-nonsense range – including great beer brewed on the premises – this has never really been a student pub, despite the sprawling accommodation blocks along the road. But a link-up with the Pack Horse near the University and the re-opening of its upstairs function toom, has seen the Fox & Newt revive its credentials as a live music venue.

Imogen's proud collection of pump clips displayed around the walls demonstrates the pub's commitment to real ale – and specifically beers from Yorkshire. "We're not about the big brands," she tells me. "We're a small freehold pub, and we like to support other small businesses."

Leeds brewpubs

THE Fox & Newt is perhaps the best-known brewpub in Leeds. Different owners have each tried to put their own stamp on the product and I remember trying a luminous green ale here once, years ago. Alumni who cut their teeth here have gone on to run bigger operations elsewhere.

Hemmed in by the narrow room, the coppers and fermenting vessels turn out two great core beers, the sessionable Brickyard Bitter and the lighter, gingery Laguna Seca. When I visited in July, production was going on side-by-side with that of the new Whippet Brewery, which is perfecting its brews here before moving to a permanent site in South Leeds.

In the first edition of this book, in 2011, only this and the **Brewery Tap** (p142) were functioning brewpubs; the heyday of the Firkin empire a fading memory. But now the addition of the **Northern Monk** (p62), **Black Swan** (p85) and **Tapped** (p131), *pictured below*, has created between them a brewpub crawl all of its own ●

Pump clips: *The Fox & Newt is committed to live music and real ale*

Veritas Ale & Wine Bar

Great George Street, LS1 3BB.
☎ **0113 242 8094**
www.markettowntaverns.co.uk

THIS is a fabulous position for a pub. Close by offices, the hospital and the law courts, it's a stone's throw from Millennium Square on a thoroughfare strewn with well-established bars and pubs.

Which all rather begs the question why it has gone through so many changes of name, image and focus over the years. It has been, by turns – and please forgive me if I've missed any or got them in the wrong order – The Waterhole, the Hogshead, the Portland and the Waterhole (again).

Several companies sniffed around the premises before it was finally reinvented as the cool and interesting Veritas late in 2010, adding a central Leeds venue to the expansive Market

Town Taverns chain. And, five years on, it seems to be thriving, and at last adding a sense of permanence to this ever-changing space.

A blackboard above the bar details the current choice of real ales, handily listing them by both strength and price. On my most recent visit I opted for a paddle of three third-pints, Timothy Taylor's smooth and easy-going Boltmaker, dark and silky Over and Stout from Goose Eye, and the Belgian-themed, slightly sour Tabatha from Partners Brewery in Dewsbury. The choice changes regularly.

The decor very much reflects the company's sombre, sober, understated themes – greys, creams and deep airforce

Truly thriving:
Veritas has had
many names
down the
years – has it
finally settled?

blues. There are wooden floors, short church pews and little stools in the pub's three main drinking spaces, while a door to the rear opens onto a private dining room perfect for parties and sociable events.

Picture windows afford views of the red brick Victorian gothic of Leeds General Infirmary, a view only partially spoiled by the hospital's grim concrete extension.

As part of the refit, one section of the bar was replaced with a glass-front fridge, well stocked with hams, pickles and tasty cheeses. Customers can use the place simply as a walk-in deli, or else sit down and try some of chef's gastropub fare alongside a pint.

Picture windows: The interior decor of Veritas is perfect for a gastropub

Market Town Taverns

TO enter one of the 15 pubs in the Market Town Taverns chain is rather like visiting one of those distressed-wood alehouses you sometimes find as life-size displays in folk museums.

Although each quite different, all bear some of this  confident company's hallmarks. The curving black-on-gold capital script is one, as are the enamelled advertising panels and framed archive posters of beers of the world.

And while there are these recognisable themes, this is no manufactured 'look' in the way that some of the bigger pub chains might set about it. Each of the Market Town Taverns has its own character, rather than some cheerless design imposed to meet the company's corporate image.

The group is behind some of the best born-again alehouses in Yorkshire. Places like **Bar T'At** in Ilkley, **Muse** in Wetherby, **Coopers** in Guiseley and – my personal favourite – Harrogate's **Old Bell**.

Each of them has been a significant addition to its local scene,

Town Hall Tavern

Westgate, LS1 2RA.
☎ 0113 244 0765
www.townhalltavernleeds.co.uk

IF you have a taste for the macabre, then the Town Hall Tavern can be an interesting place to pass an hour or so.

On the walls are pictures and cuttings on a legal theme – hanging judges, great trials and condemned men dominate and reflect this pub's traditional role as a watering hole for those engaged with the law, whether practising it, reporting it or feeling the long arm of it. Its proximity to the courts and the legal practices of nearby Park Square and Great George Street provided a ready clientele; a division into two halves meant that the law could drink on one side, the accused on the other.

Back in the market: *East of Arcadia has risen anew on a once derelict site*

but MTT has also managed to gain a reputation for making a success out of venues where previous occupants have seemingly struggled. Just as Veritas is thriving where others have failed, so the excellent **East of Arcadia** stands on the site of the miserable old Beckett's, which was allowed to slide from slow failure into dereliction.

www.markettowntaverns.co.uk

Legal theme:
Town Hall Tavern
attracts trade from
the nearby courts

Losing the screens and baffles which provided such handy intimacy has taken away some of the THT's charm and character – but the line-up of Timothy Taylor products ensures it will always be worth a visit. A short bar juts out into the room, topped by pumps dispensing Taylor's flagship brands. Wooden paddles give drinkers the opportunity to browse the range from third-pint glasses.

Along with the Old Unicorn at Bramley, the THT was once in the ownership of Dickensian-sounding pub company Musgrave and Sagar, but the pair were snapped up by the expanding Timothy Taylor pub group some years ago, which extended their empire significantly east of their heartland, which lies roughly on an axis between Skipton and Halifax. The Unicorn has now been given the Wetherspoon treatment, leaving the THT as the only Taylor's pub in the city

The floor is dark-lacquered parquet, the paintwork grey-green, ivory and deep navy blue, making interesting use of some stunning blue tiles. Leather banquettes are dotted with colouful floral cushions.

Drinks menus on each table set out the pub's impressive range – including long lists of wines, rums, vodkas, gins, and enough whiskies to keep a Scotch-lover entertained for weeks, especially those that might want to splash out £15 for a tot of the top-of-the-range Johnnie Walker Blue Label.

There's a cosmopolitan choice of bottled beers and food is served from lunchtime through to the evening daily.

Timothy Taylor Brewery

A RECENT major expansion of its Keighley Brewery has seen a significant increase in brewing capacity, yet Timothy Taylor remains wholly in family ownership and as committed as ever to the brewing traditions established during its 150-year history.

The brewery continues to use Knowle Spring Pennine water to create a wonderful range of ales which includes the refreshing and sessionable Golden Best; creamy, gentle Dark Mild; rich and toffee-ish Ram Tam; and spicy, hoppy Boltmaker, which was named Champion Beer of Britain, CAMRA's highest accolade, in 2014.

Which is to say nothing of fruity, juicy, earthy Timothy Taylor Landlord, a British brewing classic whether in bottle or on draught and a champion beer of Britain a record four times. Whatever pub I happen to be in, once my eyes are drawn to that distinctive cream and green oval pumpclip it's hard to persuade myself to try anything else.

It's the quintessential Yorkshire beer, and a case or two would probably be my Desert Island luxury, if Kirsty Young were ever to ask. The beer is central to the brewery's ambitious plans for an international export drive.

www.timothytaylor.co.uk

Mr Foley's Cask Ale House

Headrow, LS1 5RG.
☎ **0113 242 9674**
www.york-brewery.co.uk

"WE serve a bigger range of real ales than any other pub in the city centre," says manager Jason Allison, waving a proud hand across his line of twelve handpumps.

Portland stone: Mr Foley's is resident in a magnificent Headrow building

"Well, I think we do," he adds, perhaps realising the claim could lay him open to all kinds of counter-claim and retribution.

"What about the Scarb..."

"Ten," he interrupts confidently.

Jason's in the happy position of running the only York Brewery pub outside its home city, giving him more freedom to run it his own way than is afforded to those closer to base.

York beers remain the staple fare on the bar – their pale, softly bitter and refreshing Guzzler and fruity, hoppy, premium Terrier being both permanent fixtures. But the other handpumps give Jason the opportunity to put on a whole range of beers from across the country, offering his customers a broad choice of strengths and styles.

There's more. Almost 20 real ciders are arranged in boxes along the back bar, while around one hundred different bottled beers in the fridges underneath. Above, glass cabinets showcase an enviable selection of whiskies.

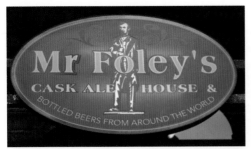

A good choice of hearty unpretentious pub meals is served on lunchtimes and evenings, Monday to Saturday.

The pub is named after Patrick James Foley, founder of the Pearl Assurance. When this Portland Stone monument first opened its doors in 1911 it was the magnificent new company headquarters. What such a building said about the company was a statement as telling as those made about the Victorian city by the grandeur of the library, art gallery and forbidding Town Hall, directly opposite.

Unlike some rather crass remodelling jobs, it was tastefully converted when it first became a pub about 15 years ago, initially as Dr Okell's. From the busy Headrow you step into a central atrium, surrounded by plush balconied areas ahead and to the right, while the left wall is dominated by the long bar.

There is some ground-level drinking space, but to access the simple comforts of tables and chairs one must ascend to the multi-levelled balconies, which in turn lead through to a quieter back room, which also benefits from wheelchair ramp access from the street behind.

From his lofty perch atop the building, flanked by two griffins, Mr Foley continues to observe the changing world below.

Brewing veteran: Martin Kellaway

Wharfe Bank Brewery

AN alumnus of Bass, Fullers and Caledonian, boss Martin Kellaway used a redundancy cheque from Heineken to strike out on his own. Just five years on, his Wharfe Bank Brewery now seems a veteran on the scene.

From an old papermill in Pool, Wharfe Bank turns out a cracking range of cask and keg ales. Regulars include the pale and easy-going Tether Blond (3.8%),

 sessionable India Pale Ale Ro Sham Bo (4.2%) and their more robust, golden and citric Yorkshire IPA (5.1%).

American-born brewer Tyler Kiley augments this roster with some diverse  specials including a Coconut Milk Stout, a Belgian Black Ale and Rhubarb Hefeweizen. One of my favourites is the rich, dark and slightly sweet Camfell Flame (4.4%).

Wharfe Bank has two pubs: the **Rook & Gaskill** is a straight-up alehouse beside York's ancient walls, while Pool's **Half Moon**, a short walk from the brewery, is essentially the brewery tap.

www.wharfebankbrewery.co.uk

The Great Leeds Pub Crawl

The Fenton

Woodhouse Lane, LS2 3ED.
☎ **0113 243 1382**
www.thefentonleeds.com

DESPITE some concessions to the students – a pool table, a juke box and a breathless programme of live music – this is recognisably the same community local which served customers from the close-knit terraces that once dominated the local landscape.

It has long been a favourite meeting place for both staff and students. In the 1950s and 60s, when Leeds University gave fellowships to rising young artists and poets, the Fenton became the place they would gravitate to, for discussions and poetry readings. Beer too, obviously.

Wandering in, you can easily imagine you have drifted back to those times. With its leather seating, glazed corridor screen, chequerboard tiled floor and old wooden panelling, its

Community local: The chequered floor of the Fenton on Woodhouse Lane

Tetley house:
*The Fenton still
displays the famous
Huntsman motif*

Variety of beers: The Fenton bar provides plenty of choice for a thirsty drinker

faded grandeur seems a better 'fit' with the staff of the two universities, than with the students. You're just as likely to bump into academics discussing their research as undergraduates talking about exams.

As the terraces were cleared and the campus expanded towards the city in the 1960s and 70s, its growth ended right at the Fenton's back door. The brutalist concrete of the physics department is now just 30 seconds' walk away from the bar. Though its famous Huntsman motif still hangs outside and is repeated in lovely old glass panels inside, you'll rarely find Tetley bitter here these days. The city's famous ale has now been supplanted by a host of offcumdens and interlopers. The choice of ales changes almost daily.

The entrance lobby is part tiled, the walls above painted a bloody crimson and stuckled up with posters for live bands. An enclosed yard has been slapped up with murals and decked out with chairs and tables to create an unlikely urban beer garden and a welcome haven for the smokers.

Screen time: *Customers can also enjoy a beer garden and music room upstairs*

The students often gravitate to a room across the corridor which is dominated by the pool table and juke box, while an untidy heap of board games offers further distractions. The Fenton's chief credential as a student pub comes when bands take to the upstairs stage, which is more nights than not. It's the penultimate stop on the Otley Run too, so by the time the fancy-dress pub crawlers reach here, they're usually blathered.

The Otley Run

WOODIES in Far Headingley is the starting point of the city's most infamous pub crawl. On almost every day of the week, groups in fancy dress attempt this marathon drinking session, which takes in every pub along the Otley Road – and a few just off it – between Far Headingley and the city centre.

The accepted route is **Woodies**, **Three Horseshoes**, **New Inn**, **Arcadia** (no fancy dress allowed), **Headingley Taps**, **Arc**, **Box**, **Skyrack**, **Original Oak**, **Hyde Park**, **Library**, **Pack Horse**, **Eldon**, **Fenton** and **Dry Dock**.

It's quite a long walk – the stretches either side of the Hyde Park are occasionally done by bus – and the better-organised groups have a designated timekeeper to keep drinkers to schedule.

Skyrack and Original Oak:
The two pubs stand directly opposite each other in central Headingley, close to the bulk of student accommodation. Their names both recall the ancient 'Scir Ac' – or Shire Oak – under which meetings were held in medieval times. The Oak stood here for hundreds of years, before collapsing during a gale in 1941.

Men behaving badly: *The author, front, with friends Scott, Jon and Tom, having a quiet night out on the Otley Run.*

Few students at the city's three Universities manage to reach the end of their studies without attempting at least one Otley Run, for some it is a termly ritual. For many of the city's sixth formers, it has become the standard rite-of-passage on turning 18. It can get very messy ●

Starting point:
Woodies Ale House

The Great Leeds Pub Crawl

Old Bar

Lifton Place, LS2 9JZ.
☎ **0113 380 1400**
www.luu.org.uk/building/oldbar/

THE bars and nightclubs of Leeds University's union building make this a popular destination for students and locals alike. The suntrap Terrace Bar is a popular summer venue, though its lack of anything more interesting than smoothflow ales on the bar requires the more discerning drinker to head downstairs to the Old Bar.

When former students return to Leeds, this is the one place which they almost invariably want to visit. When recent plans were announced for a major refit of the union building, the students were determined the Old Bar should stay the same.

It was founded in 1939 and has been a popular meeting place for generations ever since, providing an education in northern culture every bit as valid as anything which happens in the Uni's classrooms, lecture halls and laboratories.

That education begins the moment you arrive at the bar and are faced with eight real ale handpulls, many offering beers from Yorkshire breweries. Cask Marque status – rare for a student bar – acknowledges this commitment to great beer; the

Union building:
The University can boast several popular bars and nighclubs, but the downstairs Old Bar is best for the discerning drinker

union's lively real ale society would be quick to flag any reduction in quality.

With regular quizzes, live gigs, Sky Sports TV, some quality pub grub and regular food and drink festivals, this is very much a community local right in the heart of campus.

The Refectory

JUST along from the student union, a blue plaque outside the refectory recalls Valentine's Day 1970, when The Who's seminal album *Live at Leeds* was recorded in this cavernous student venue.

For three decades from the mid-sixties onwards, the refectory hosted a regular programme of concerts which reads like a *Who's Who* of rock nobility. Acts like Led Zeppelin, Pink Floyd, the Rolling Stones, Genesis, and Deep Purple all played here. Now rarely used for concerts, the refectory remains worth a visit, if only for the exhibition which lists every gig held here, alongside stunning monochrome photographs from those remarkable times ●

Star attraction: Elton John, the Clash, the Stranglers and Siouxsie and the Banshees are among the acts with performances celebrated in the Refectory

Cask commitment:
The Eldon serves choice

The Great Leeds Pub Crawl

▌ The Eldon

Woodhouse Lane, LS2 9DX.
☎ **0113 245 3591**
www.johnbarras.com

IT's 11.05am, Thursday 9 July 2015, and I'm sitting with a glass of Leeds Pale in the Eldon as the morning sunshine gushes in from Woodhouse Lane, where urgent traffic thrums along outside.

Whatever assumptions you make about someone who makes a living from writing about beer, I ought to say that a morning beer is still, for me, a rarity. But the second day of a compelling Ashes Test series allows me to break this little rule.

Bang opposite the sprawling engineering department, this has long been a favourite pub with university staff and students, its multi-screen Sky TV coverage, decent choice of real ales and cheap and cheerful pub meals make this a popular mainstream spot both at lunch and at the end of the working day. And, close to the end of the Otley Run (see p168), it attracts a lively straggle

Sporting congregation: Multi-screen television coverage is widely popular

Sports pubs

THERE is something rather special about watching the football in the pub, joining a few mates to cheer on the Rhinos, or catching a few overs of the Test match on your lunch hour. It doesn't match being there, of course it doesn't, but it scores heavily over the solitary experience of watching at home.

In our insular and increasingly secular society there is something profound about sharing such moments – whether in victory or defeat – in a congregation. It's almost spiritual.

While many pubs offer Sky and BT Sport coverage, a few like the **Eldon** and the **Old Bar** (p170) have put it absolutely at the heart of their business. Close to Headingley Stadium, both **Box** and the **Headingley Taps** compete for trade, while **Shooters Sports Bar** in the Headrow is another, though the choice of beers is nothing to write home about.

Better is the **Brotherhood** in New Briggate, where displays of sporting memorabilia dominate the decor at a lively pub which is also a big part of the local nightscene in this burgeoning part of town.

Followers of the racing should head for the **Templar** (p193), while **The Albert** in Yeadon, **147 Sports Bar** in Pudsey, **Devon** in Crossgates and **Fleece** at Farsley provide sports pubs for their respective suburbs, just as the **Roundhay**, **Horsforth** and **Hyde Park** each do in theirs ●

of inebriated fancy dressers as the evenings wear on.

Though the locals are a welcome source of trade, this pub's fortunes inevitably ebb and flow with the academic tide. Packed as the exams finish, it can be deserted a week later, after the students have returned home.

But unlike many in this marketplace, the Eldon makes a real commitment to cask ale, with six handpulls on the bar, and blackboards chalked up with the current choices and those next to arrive. Some of the better-known local brewers – the likes of Kirkstall, Leeds, Ilkley and Timothy Taylor's – are often represented. In similar vein, the menu offers straight-up pub grub value – burgers, steaks and pies.

So, nothing especially surprising here. The Eldon is very much a mainstream pub that is doing steady and unsurprising business. Aside from my shameful morning boozing, that is.

Oldest pub: The Pack Horse, now and then...

The Pack Horse

Woodhouse Lane, LS2 9DX.
☎ **0113 245 3980**

A NEW dartboard was long-serving licensee Paul McIntyre's slightly ironic response to a £300,000 refurbishment at the cavernous Library across the road.

Established in the mid-18th century, the Pack Horse is comfortably Woodhouse's oldest pub and one of its interesting old images around the walls shows the Pack Horse around 1850, with working men, top-hatted gents and girls in pretty dresses arranged outside. A sign over the door names Benjamin Jubb as landlord and proclaims his licence to brew and sell his own beers and wines on the premises.

The pub is essentially in the same place, but back then was at right angles to the main road. It was rebuilt and re-orientated around one hundred years ago.

Mr Jubb may be long gone, but the pub still sells its own beer, with two ales from its stablemate Fox & Newt (p150) sold alongside two or three guest beers from the Punch Taverns roster.

With its distressed wood, tiling and old leather banquettes, the simple, slightly shabby, down-at-heel Pack Horse is the antithesis to the big-spending Library. It's well known for its music, with a concert room upstairs available for hire by local bands. Cheap and cheerful food, including a Sunday carvery, keep punters coming through the door.

Paul has been in the Pack Horse for 15 years, meaning he has probably served more Otley Run (p168) participants than anyone. By the time the fancy dress pub crawlers reach the Pack Horse, they are fairly well-oiled, having started the rite-of-passage trek in Far Headingley some hours earlier.

"It used to be all students when I first started, but that's changed now, you get office trips, birthday groups, anyone. People look up 'what to do in Leeds' online and it's on there. It's become an all-year thing now; summer Saturdays can be really busy."

Bullseye: *Pack Horse proprietor Paul McIntyre*

177

The Great Leeds Pub Crawl

Ship-shape:
The Dry Dock

Detours

PERHAPS it should come as no surprise that there are so many licensed premises close to the University campus – but this route of nine pubs could easily have been a good deal longer.

As well as the Old Bar, the student union is home to a number of bars and clubs, with the broad outside drinking space at the **Terrace Bar** a popular summer drinking spot.

Between here and the Fox & Newt is the excellent **Faversham** in Mount Preston Street which manages to please both staff and students by offering quality lunchtime dining and then mutating by night into a popular venue for DJs and live music.

The live music **Well** is a short hop from here too, and visiting Veritas and the wonderful Victoria affords the opportunity for a long Great George Street crawl (see page 39). After Foley's you could take a short walk to **Around The World In Eighty Beers** which serves an appropriately cosmopolitan selection.

Directly opposite Leeds Beckett University is the beached barge of the **Dry Dock**, while further up the road is the student-themed **Library**. Both are in the Mitchell's and Butler's Scream chain. ●

Excellent:
The Faversham

Northern
Quarter

The Great Leeds Pub Crawl

THE city's centre of gravity seems in constant flux. In the Millennium's first decade it seemed to shift decisively towards Call Lane and the riverside, yet more recently some exciting things have been happening at the other end of Briggate.

Though bars like **Reliance**, **North**, **MOJO** and **Sandinista** have been here a while, new places like **Social**, **Belgrave**, **Pit** and **Manahatta** have given an extra interest to the city's Northern Quarter. The recent arrival of **Shuffledog** in the curve-fronted Crispin Lofts on the corner of North Street and New York Road really cements this as a serious circuit.

This crawl also takes in two of the more venerable pubs on the Leeds scene, the lovely old **Wrens**, whose fortunes have always been tied to those of the Grand Theatre nearby, and the architecturally interesting **Templar**, a sociable haven whose long-term future remains in doubt.

Street style: *Outdoor drinking is a big part of the city's Northern Quarter*

Curtain-up: The Wrens is a very popular venue with theatre-goers

The Wrens Hotel

New Briggate, LS2 8JD.
☎ **0113 245 8888**
www.thewrenshotel.co.uk

IT was deep into Wimbledon fortnight when I called in at the Wrens. Brit James Ward was battling gamely on Court One, and a group of ladies-who-lunch had one eye on the tennis and another on the splendid afternoon tea which they had just been served: dainty sandwiches on a three-tier cake rack, tea served from an ornate teapot and mountainous slices of cake.

Afternoon tea is just one of the points of difference at a pub which has had numerous changes of decor and direction over the years, yet remained popular with theatre-goers who find this the ideal pre- and post-performance watering hole.

It is named after founder Alfred Wren, this once common method of naming pubs applies also to a few others in this guide including the Scarbrough and Whitelock's – and more recently, Jake's Bar.

Once a Tetley pub pure and simple, it now offers up to five real ales – Leeds Brewery's excellent malty Vienna mild was my choice on this occasion – as well as some quality meals in its intimate dining area to the rear.

I don't miss the tired, grimy alehouse feel it once had – its toilets were the worst in Leeds – yet it's hard to escape the conclusion that much of the Wrens' charm and character has been lost in successive refurbishments. Now it almost feels like a lesson in neutrality, with bland magnolia walls rising above sage green panelling.

Beautiful monochrome images of the city do provide an interesting distraction, all the same.

Theatre Pubs

DRINKING and drama go together, they always have. Plenty of pubs in cities and towns around the country have relied on the trade of thespians and theatricals, producers and paying public.

The Wrens is a case in point. It has long been a favourite of members of the Opera North company, and of the Grand Theatre audience. It's close enough to nip out here in the interval, throw down a pint, and be back in time for curtain up on the second half.

If anything, links between the **White Swan** (see page 32) and the City Varieties are stronger. The pub dates back to the early 18th century, and by 1765 this old coaching inn had expanded to incorporate a singing room. Around a century later the popularity of the entertainment here was sufficient to persuade owner Charles Thornton – of Thornton's Arcade fame – to convert the upstairs into Thornton's New Music Hall.

In the 1890s, the **Scarbrough** (see page 124) was owned by Fred Wood, who also owned Leeds City Varieties. Winning acts from the pub's

Cavern of pleasures: *Belgrave Music Hall and Canteen is an absolute delight*

talent contests were transferred across town to the theatre's stage.

This very British tradition continues. The bars around Millennium Square welcome pre and post–performance audiences from the Carriageworks Theatre; in Chapel Allerton, **Seven Arts** does good food and hand–pulled ale – plus an eclectic range of music, drama, film and comedy in its intimate rear theatre space ●

Belgrave Music Hall and Canteen

Cross Belgrave Street, LS2 8JP.
☎ **0113 234 6160**
www.belgravemusichall.com

IT took me a while to really catch up with this place. Honestly, I found the name off-putting, the subliminal power of suggestion telling me this was all about bands and burgers, DJs and daiquiris.

When I finally walked through the door, one spring afternoon some six months after they were first opened, I realised how stupidly blinkered I had been. To stroll through a lazy sunlit city, to close off the working day in this scruffy cavern of pleasures was as near to heaven as I could reasonably demand.

I've been in at least ten times since.

The eclectic choice of beer came as the single biggest surprise in an afternoon of little epiphanies. A long bar topped with a great choice of cask and craft keg ales stretches down the right-hand side, flying in the face of my outdated prejudice that those coming to watch live music don't much care what they're drinking so long as it's cold and wet.

Across the room, heavy steel-framed windows speak of this building's industrial past. But when I came here some time in the eighties, this was Ike's Bistro, all burritos and Budweiser.

It's been a few things since and plenty of others before. The latest refit has seen it stripped back to its barest essentials, this old building's commercial past celebrated in utilitarian industrial design. Those old windows may have been slapped

Long bar: *The latest Belgrade re-fit has stripped the building down to its roots*

up in battleship enamel, but there are hints of rust on the tables' heavy-forged ironwork, white glazed tiles like you'd get in factory toilets and benches fashioned from oak slabs thick as railway sleepers.

Badly pointed brickwork is interrupted by a small patch of breeze blocks, lathered with emulsion and stuckled up with flyers for the latest gigs. In an era where style is too often prized higher than content, all this, the cheap particle boarding of the bar front, the old school chairs, the tatty mismatched sofas, each speak of a bar happy just the way it is.

Up on the roof:
...at the Belgrade

Rooftop drinking

IF you walk through the double doors at the back of the **Belgrave**, and up a three-storey string of claustrophobic stairways heavy in gothic black, you emerge onto a broad roof terrace decked out in a garage sale of garden furniture, high above the traffic.

The Belgrave is one of the few pubs able to offer rooftop drinking in a city which may not have the majesty of central London, nor the glass and concrete splendour of Manhattan, yet still offers some arresting views of its own.

The **Alchemist** and **Angelica** exploit their elevated position to provide balcony views around the Trinity Quarter. **Slate** has nice views of historic St John's Church, though it's hard to imagine anywhere to beat the panoramic views from the **Sky Lounge** of the Mint Hotel ●

EST. 2002

SANDINISTA

NUEST

Revolutionary:
Sandinista in Cross
Belgrave Street

EST. 2002

SANDI

Sandinista

Cross Belgrave Street, LS2 8JP
☎ **0113 243 0395**
www.sandinista.co.uk

THERE used to be an exclamation mark after the name, but this was presumably removed in the same refit that saw the wonderful mural of Paul Simonon wrecking his bass guitar buried under a layer of mucky yellow paint.

If all this stands for something, it's perhaps that now Sandinista is moving into second decade maturity, it's no longer as punk as it used to be.

The choice of biographies – Dylan, Led Zeppelin, Keith Richards among them – the eclectic playlist and the arresting display of classic rock posters on the stairway, suggest that a bar named after one of punk's great albums is

Blind Tyger

UPSTAIRS from Sandinista, and run by the same company, is the excellent Blind Tyger, arguably the best cocktail bar at this end of town.

With a touch more formality than the easy-going, casual feel of its much-loved neighbour downstairs, Blind Tyger styles itself as a drinking den, where great beers, fine wines and select spirits collide with soul, laid-back blues and prohibition jazz.

There's something of the William Morris to the design; booths can be booked; the whole place can be hired for rather special occasions.

To drink here is almost to feel part of some exclusive little club, known only to the cognoscenti, available just to a favoured few.

www.blindtyger.co.uk

now happy to embrace guitar music's mainstream. In keeping with its positioning as a Cantina Bar, the food is mostly tapas.

The central bar serves two distinct drinking spaces one of which transforms magically into a music and dance venue late on, the tables whisked down through a trap door while the DJ booth is cranked into life. A single handpull was on this occasion offering Fell Brewery's lovely amber Triple-A ale, but craft keg and bottled beers extend the choice. I passed an enjoyable half

All grown up: Sandinista

hour with the excellent golden Uncertainty Principle IPA from Atom brewery in Hull

Its outdoor tables are a great place to drink on a sunny afternoon, but Sandinista is better after dark when they light the candles and the huge picture windows offer a surprising panorama of floodlit buildings, hypnotic tail lights and twinkling tungsten.

Sandinista remains fiercely non-conformist, heavily committed to local charities and community action and more choosy than most bars about the brands stocked behind its bar. It remains true to its owners' Bohemian vision of an ethically-driven, ethnically-diverse business – the juices Cuban, the coffees Nicaraguan, the tea, sugar and hot chocolate all Fairtrade.

Mind you, it does seem strange that a bar which supports homelessness charity Simon On The Streets can no longer find a home for Simonon The Bassist.

The Reliance

North Street, LS2 7PN.
☎ **0113 295 6060**
www.the-reliance.co.uk

THE Reliance's attractive frontage of tall windows curving around a street corner, sits a little off the beaten track in North Street, some fifty yards beyond the inner ring road.

It is a perennial favourite on the Leeds bar scene; its quality beer and proper pub food continue to attract a big following.

189

The Great Leeds Pub Crawl

High culture: The food and intimate ambience draw a discerning crowd

Being slightly detached, it's not on the main shopping or pedestrian routes and not easily driven to unless you know exactly where you're going. I'm sure that plenty who tread the popular circuit of North Bar, MOJO and Sandinista never actually find their way here.

Instead the Reli attracts a slightly older crowd, some who will spend the whole evening here, others who might be nipping off for some high culture at the Grand.

It has a cool feel of faded elegance to it, with its high ceilings, gnarled floorboards and simple colour scheme of creams, deep reds and greens. Flickering tea lights add to the intimacy.

Drinkers and diners share big, solid oak tables and chairs, while a room to the right of the main entrance has some comfy leather sofas, and a short flight of stairs beside the bar leads up to a dining room at the back, where you can watch your meals being prepared in the open-plan kitchen.

The fare is neatly tailored for its slightly more discerning

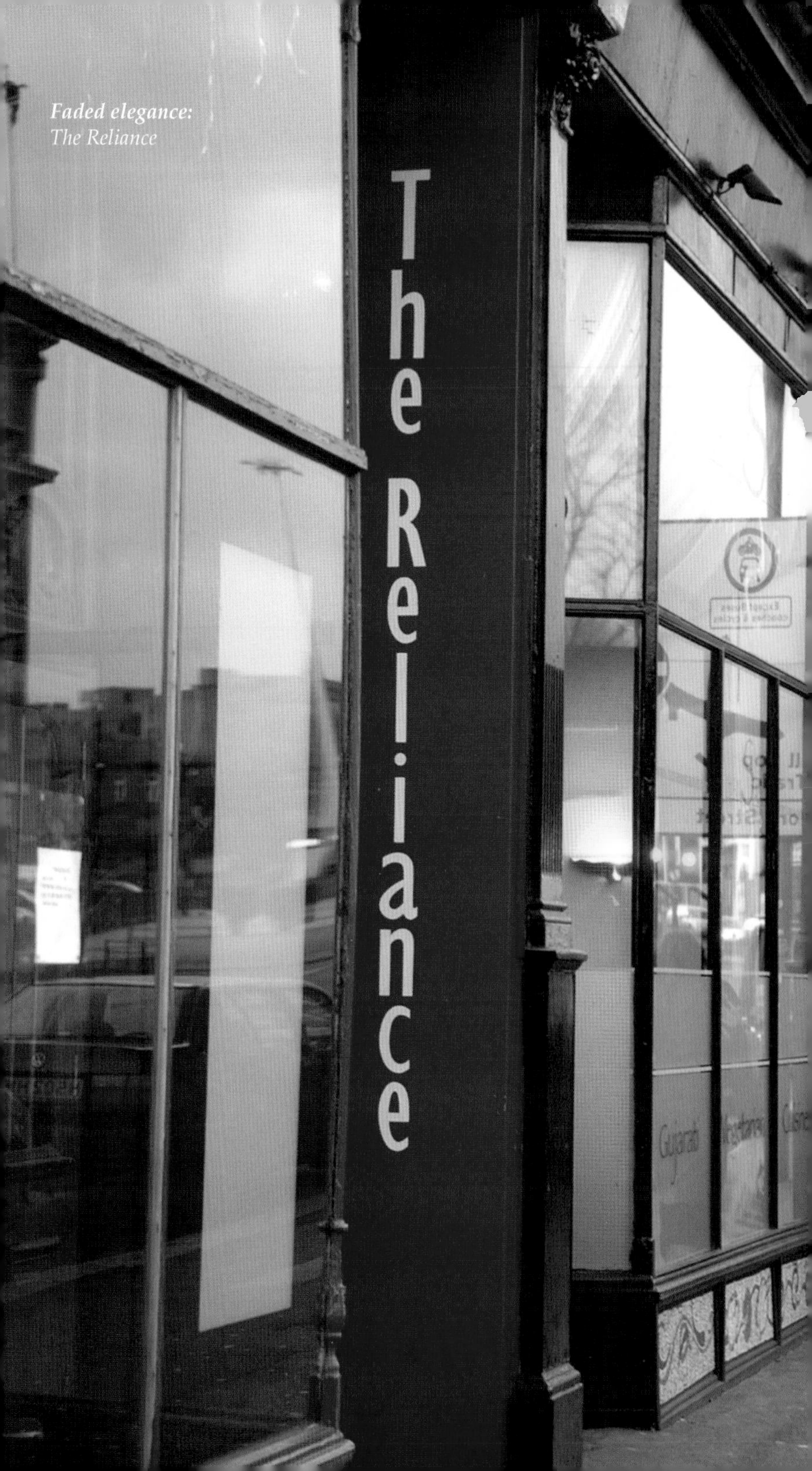

Faded elegance:
The Reliance

market, and that starts from the moment you pitch up at a bar bristling with great beers – an eclectic choice of keg and bottled ales augments an ever-changing selection of hand-pulled real ales. Barnsley's excellent Acorn Brewery produce the refreshing Reliance Best, while Knaresborough's Roosters has a permanent place on the bar.

A pre-theatre menu offers a fixed-price three course menu, if you don't mind snoring your way through *Rigoletto*.

Roosters Brewery

IT's possible that 2015 will be remembered as the Year of the Can.

Once considered the packaging of choice for the nasty end of the market, canned beers – notably US imports – have been rediscovered by brewers and drinkers alike.

Not least by Roosters, who have installed a new kit in their Knaresborough Brewery to start canning some of their award-winning beers.

It's entirely fitting that Roosters should be in the British vanguard of this little revolution. America has long been a major influence on business here.

The burgeoning craft beer scene stateside, with its emphasis on heroic levels of hop content, was a big influence on founder Sean Franklin, who gave these styles a distinctive Yorkshire twist.

Everyone's doing it now, but back in 1993 this was a radical innovation.

Sean has moved on, but the brewery has continued in that vein, now owned by former Market Town Taverns boss Ian Fozard, and run by his sons Tom and Oliver.

Fulsome, fruity and deeply refreshing Yankee (4.3%) remains the flagship ale, while coffee–accented Londinium Porter (5.5%) and determinedly bitter Fort Smith (5%) add variety to the range.

If I had to choose a favourite it might be aromatic, fruity, bitter, golden Baby Faced Assassin IPA (6.1%). There's a really enticing tropical fruit blast to the aroma, which continues into a complex taste, heavy with mango and oranges, but so delightfully easy drinking that its gentleness offers a false sense of security.

www.roosters.co.uk

Glorious frontage: The Templar is one of the great city centre public houses

Templar Hotel

Templar Street, LS2 7NU.
☎ **0113 243 0318**
www.johnbarras.com

WHEN people talk of Leeds's great old city centre pubs, overwhelmingly the list centres on a square mile south of Millennium Square, which takes in the Victoria and Whitelock's, the Ship and the Adelphi.

Which does a great disservice to the faded grandeur of the Templar, whose stained and leaded glass, dark oak beams, mirrors and polished oak panelling lend the feel of a gentlemen's private club. This is particularly so in its square rear snug, where comfy green banquettes, a red-tiled fireplace and displays of old crockery make for a civilised place to drink.

The long main bar is livelier, with sociable booths, topped

New and old: Slot machines and cosy nooks in the Templar Hotel

by panels of stained glass. Around the walls a series of pictures and displays tell the history of the pub and of the Knights Templar, the feared fighting Crusaders dubbed "The Army of God" by one early Pope. Though their fame was forged in the

Holy Land it should be no surprise that they are remembered in the name of a Leeds pub and the street it stands upon. The Templars owned vast swathes of Yorkshire, including Temple Newsam estate in east Leeds.

For those regular customers of a certain age who find little for themselves in the bars which have sprung up nearby, this must seem a perfect haven from the cares of the world outside. Sky Sports offers a further point of distinction.

It remains a proud purveyor of great beer, with eight cask ales, including a special Templar Ale brewed by Ridgeside in Meanwood to highlight the potential threat to the future of this great old pub.

*Under threat:
Wrecking balls*

To those determined to deliver a glossy future for this rather neglected part of town, this old-style alehouse with its ornate facade of Burmantoft tiles must seem a tick on the skin of their brave new world.

Their bulldozers are making steady progress up Eastgate; the flagship John Lewis store is due to open in 2016. And at the north-western tip of the site lies this oak-panelled paradise. Though city planners wisely listened to CAMRA's protests, obliging the developer to maintain the building and secure the "continuous running of the business in its current format," it's not hard to conceive of a stray wrecking ball conveniently wiping this grand old jewel off the map.

Melbourne Brewery

THOUGH the Templar dates back to the early 19th century, its red, green and ivory frontage are from 1927, a legacy of its time in the Melbourne Brewery chain.

It's more than 50 years since

Melbourne was subsumed into the Tetley's empire, yet at the Templar, the Palace and a fair few other pubs around West Yorkshire, there are plenty of reminders of that famous old name.

The mosaic at Tong Road's much-missed Beech is a rarity, but in several other pubs the Melbourne Ales name remains in block letters above the door, the company's distinctive logo of a red-and-gold cloaked bowing courtier still visible in the original windows.

Melbourne, based in Regent Street, was originally the Leeds and Wakefield Breweries Company. It is perhaps credit to Tetley that, once these pubs changed hands in the 1960s, they didn't set about erasing the name of their former rival. Perhaps they had better things to do ●

Reflected cool:
MOJO rocks

MOJO

Merrion Street, LS1 6PQ.
☎ 0113 244 6387
www.mojobar.co.uk

IF you're looking for draught beer, don't bother with MOJO, which doesn't sell a single one, not even a draught lager. And if you like your bars to look good from the outside, or have stunning panoramic views from their front windows, you'd probably best give this place a miss as well, given its location down the narrow, lightless and slightly seedy end of Merrion Street.

Yet to leave MOJO out from any trawl around the licensed premises of Leeds would be to omit a bar which over the past 20 years has helped define the city's whole drinking culture.

MOJO combines something of the slightly shabby chic of a New York drinking den with the musical memorabilia of a Hard Rock Cafe, and for me at least, its compelling combination of music, cocktails, lager and sheer atmosphere makes it the daddy of the Leeds bar scene.

There might be few beers on display here, but the fridges always hold curious cosmopolitan delights. The Brooklyn lager served in an ice-cold glass sure hit the spot on my summertime visit. Its cocktail list brims with old favourites and new creations, and with its endlessly fascinating collection of rock photographs and concert posters, louche-living MOJO remains a great place.

To drink here is to bask in the reflected cool of Bob Marley and Neil Young, Pink Floyd and Patti Smith, the Beatles and the Stones.

I like it best just after opening, when you can get served without having to fight through the crowds to reach the bar, when you can find a seat, or wander around those fantastic photographs, listen to the music and enjoy a quiet conversation.

Pub with no beer:
...but plenty of spirit

As evening drifts into night the bar becomes louder, the soundtrack harder, the pace of life that bit more frantic.

Boss Mal Evans is the cocktail guru, and has added some distinctive signature drinks to a list which also features classics like the Rum Punch, the Daiquiri and the Caipirinha. The Harlem Mugger reads like a shopping list for a trip to the off-licence – vodka, gin, rum, Cointreau, Kahlúa, Grand Marnier, Prosecco and cranberry.

Merrion Street

NOW closed to traffic in drinking hours, Merrion Street has taken the opportunity to embrace the outdoos with each bar colonizing the cobbles with windbreaks and furniture.

Where once **MOJO** dominated, there is now a little bar crawl all of its own, with Merrion Street the Northern Quarter's equivalent of the bar-saturated Call Lane, half a mile south of here. You might start at **Verve**, stylish and cool with some fabulous beers, including a clutch of worthily-famous Belgians, as well as free live music and comedy, plus a weekend tequila bar.

Styled as a 'Deep South Dive Bar', **Mean Eyed Cat** is opening in autumn 2015 in the premises formerly known as **Reform**.

Across the road is **Pit** (overleaf) as well as the New York–inspired **Manahatta**. Cocktails and quality wines predominate in this cavernous two-storey venue, another from the Arc Inspirations group.

Recent arrival **Soba** fuses east and west: Pan-Asian street food colliding with cocktails in a formula perfected over the past decade and a half in its sister bars in Glasgow and Edinburgh ●

Avuncular boss:
Mal Evans

The Great Leeds Pub Crawl

▎ The Pit

Merrion Street, LS1 6PQ.
☎ 0113 247 0601
www.arcinspirations.com

THEY call it The King, and it's one of the more intriguing items on the menu at the Pit.

This Elvis tribute combines his 'favourite foods' – a giant burger slapped up with cheese, bacon and strawberry jam in a doughnut topped with peanut butter. It's an interesting collision between the savoury and the sweet, but I couldn't have one often.

The American influence is something of a theme at the Pit, where the menu reflects traditional cowboy cooking – dig pit, light fire, cook meat.

A hand-built Oklahoma smoker recreates the whole backwoods experience on a menu where ribs, wings, burgers, steaks predominate.

One nice touch is that 25p from each sale of the entry-level Lighthouse Burger goes to the Lighthouse School in Leeds – Britain's first special free school for children with autism.

Northern Quarter

The modest Merrion Street frontage belies the cavernous space within. Stepping down the stairs you reach an atmospheric bar of post-industrial chic – rough concrete pillars, aircon ducting and metal factory lights – softened by some attractive wooden panelling.

Soft music pulses through the place, becoming louder and more insistent as the day wears on. Rows of comfortable leather-backed booths offer a sociable place to eat and drink.

Curving around one corner of the main room, an attractive, colourful bar is topped by fonts dispensing a changing choice of craft ales, including Kolsch-influenced Pit Canary, the gently hoppy refreshing house beer specially brewed by the sublimely innovative Thornbridge Brewery in Derbyshire.

The Pit experience can also be enjoyed at Stainbeck Lane in Chapel Allerton and The Ginnel in Harrogate.

Arc Inspirations

PIT is one of the newer brands in the Arc Inspirations chain, whose monosyllabic outlets Box and Arc have occasionally been joined by those afforded a second vowel – Napa, Trio, Banyan.

The group was among the first to see Chapel Allerton's potential for bar culture, turning end–of–parade premises which had been a French restaurant and an American diner into Zed, which led the remarkable changes in this once–sleepy suburb. Now renamed Kith and Kin, it reopened in autumn 2015.

Headingley is another stronghold for the group, where they trade high on students, pre–club drinkers and Otley runners.

Arc has embraced craft beer, notably from the US, and pioneered the Schooner movement, dispensing beers into two–thirds–pint glasses.

"The trend is away from cask ale," Arc boss Martin Wolstencroft tells me. "You'll never satisfy CAMRA's diehards, but the craft beer range is now so broad you can cater for all tastes and guarantee consistency."

www.arcinspirations.com

North Bar

New Briggate, LS1 6NU.
☎ 0113 242 4540
www.northbar.com

NORTH is an absolute institution on the city bar scene. A catalyst for developing this once-neglected part of town as a haven of bar culture, this long, narrow, often rather cramped bar can still spring a surprise with its choice of beers, and is always worth a visit.

It is the range of beers which has made this place such a favourite on the circuit. The UK's first draught Erdinger, Sierra Nevada and Brooklyn Lager were all poured at North. Inspired by Belgians Chimay and Duvel, and American

Anchor Brewery, directors John Gyngell and Christian Townsley were determined to continually give their customers something new, unfamiliar and interesting.

The selection, both on the bar and in the amply-stocked double-fronted fridges behind, is refreshed on a regular basis, though you can generally expect to find lagers from Germany, Italy and the Low Countries, plenty of bottled beers from around the globe, draught Krieks and Framboises.

The decor is deceptively simple, with light green walls and a parquet floor, leather stools against a purple-fronted bar. Little of the natural light from Briggate penetrates to the back of the long bar. Around the walls are dotted a range of original artworks – North doubles as a gallery, allowing local artists to show off their skills.

New lanterns over the bar, and the addition of a slatted

wooden suspended ceiling have given a softer edge to a bar which might sometimes feel a little spartan and soulless. It packs a great atmosphere once the beer starts flowing and the noise levels increase.

Relaxed cool – The North Bar

North Bar opened in 1997 and featured some curious choices like Beamish Red, Guinness and Fosters. The selection has improved somewhat down the years, while the group has spread out its little revolution from Briggate to trade on a mix of cosmopolitan beers and an atmosphere of relaxed cool in a few select venues.

Despite the huge changes all around in the decade and more since North first opened its doors, it remains unspoiled, unpretentious, and true to its mission of bringing great beer to the people of Leeds. The "We Love Beer" neon sign over the bar sums it up perfectly.

Golden Owl Brewery

NORTH Bar was one of the first to serve beers from the Golden Owl Brewery, named in honour of the dramatic Civic Hall sculptures.

Even so, the brewery is more of a cuckoo than an owl, without its own premises yet developing its beers using spare capacity at other brewers. It's a common practice. Northern Monk did the same; Whippet and Wharfe Bank both began at the Burley Street Brewery before establishing their own sites.

The only one I have so far tried is a 5.5% ABV Golden Owl Pale which explodes with a big fruity blast of Columbus and Galaxy hops, but they also do a 4.8% Pale and a 6% Saison. A little quiet of late, a recent tweet on Twitter suggested that brewing would resume soon. Bars such as Chapel Allerton's **Pit**, the **Stew & Oyster** in Oakwood and **Outlaws Yacht Club** in New York Street are all occasional stockists.

goldenowlbrewery.co.uk

Just to be sociable;
A lovely little bar

SOCIAL

CASK ALES

FRESH COFFEE

HOMEMADE
STEW

The Great Leeds Pub Crawl

Social Bar

Merrion Street, LS2 8JG.
☎ **0113 244 1635**

TWO handpumps and fonts dispensing craft ales and some non-standard lagers are the chief attractions of this lovely little bar close to the busy junction of Merrion Street and New Briggate.

But its rear beer garden provides a surprising suntrap, while its piano and football table offer further indoor distractions.

The real ales change regularly but Revolution Brewery's lime and coriander witbier The Message and Fullers' Seafarer were the choice during my visit here in July. The latter proved welcome relief from the roiling heatwave outside; passing cars encouraged a steady breeze to sweep through the open doors.

Like at the nearby Belgrave, the decor is post-industrial chic. A simple colour scheme of green and cream is splashed across the plaster, the side walls stripped back to attractive red brick.

Flower power:
The Social Bar decor is best described as being post-industrial chic

Simple furniture: school chairs, pine tables and a brace of leather sofas provide an unpretentious place to drink. Single-stem flowers are thrust into beer bottles on each table. Its relaxed atmosphere draws an eclectic clientele.

Once an antique shop, these premises had several incarnations as bars of various persuasion before being taken over by the Brudenell in 2014. "We've just tried to keep it simple," says manager Aaron Patterson. "I think a lot of bars are going the same way."

The Great Leeds Pub Crawl

Georgian stalwart: The Eagle has long been renowned for its real ale

Detours

THERE are plenty of alternatives for anyone wishing to extend this pub crawl a little further, even aside from the clutch of bars on Merrion Street (see page 199).

A couple of doors down from North is the dimly-lit stairwell which leads to the subterranean **Sela Bar**, where a short bar counter is crammed with an excitingly continental range of beers, which go great with their famous pizzas.

Further along is the sporty-themed **Brotherhood**, while for beers, boogie and burgers you might head across the road to the **It Bar**. Dotted around the Merrion Centre, the varied pleasures of the lively **Merchant**, **Picture House** carvery and **Stick or Twist** Wetherspoons lie in wait.

Just along from the Reliance the new BrewDog bar **Shuffledog** opened in the summer of 2015 in the grandiose Crispin Lofts. This is all a far cry from when North Street was dominated by two great old pubs.

The old Irish pub the White Stag was pulled down years ago and while the real ale haven of **The Eagle** is not the shining star it was, it remains worthy of a visit, not least because this fine Georgian building is one of the oldest unaltered pubs in the city ●

Further Afield

The Great Leeds Pub Crawl

Beyond the city: *The Fox & Hounds at Bramhope is one pub among hundreds*

BEYOND the city centre, pub culture thrives in all its glorious forms. From simple one-room taverns to open-plan family dining houses, drinking dens to community social clubs, the city suburbs and the outlying towns of the LS postcodes have plenty to offer the serious drinker.

Here we visit just a handful, but there were plenty more I might easily have included. The Prospect at Hunslet, the Fleece at Farsley, Fox & Hounds at Bramhope and the Red Lion at Shadwell are among the most signal omissions, but it would have taken me another year and a book the size of the *Yellow Pages* to have visited them all.

But this chapter offers a flavour of what's out there, with some of the best suburban venues such as Kirkstall's Bridge and Woodhouse's Chemic, some great local pub crawls in Horsforth, Meanwood and Chapel Allerton, and a look at the thriving pub and brewing scene in Otley and Wetherby.

The Abbey Inn

Pollard Lane, Newlay, LS13 1EQ.
☎ 0113 258 1248

IN the spring of 2015, Martin Lockett picked up the award for the city's most improved pub, from the local branch of CAMRA.

Richly deserved, the award marks a major turnaround for a pub which had been lurching disappointingly downhill for a while. Its place in the *Good Beer Guide* had gone, its county Pub of the Year title a fading memory.

Manager Martin's return after a spell out of the business has seen him get the Abbey back on the map. "It has been a turbulent period," he admits. "But now we have a team which people recognise; they talk to the customers, they say 'goodbye' when you leave. These little things are very important."

They are, not least because this pub is at an absolute dead end, won't get any passing trade – save for the occasional walker – and for the Abbey to thrive, Martin needs to persuade punters to make the awkward trek down Pollard Lane from Bramley Fall Park to this famous old inn.

Its history is probably unique. It began life as a farmhouse in the 18th century, but by 1826 it was already an inn and

Most improved: *Abbey manager Martin Lockett, left, receives CAMRA's award from branch chairman Mike Hampshire*

The Great Leeds Pub Crawl

Haunted pubs

FOR many years **The Abbey** doubled as a mortuary. The bodies, often suicide victims pulled from the canal and river nearby, were laid out in the back room. Perhaps unsurprisingly, ghosts abound: a grey lady, a Cavalier and a mysterious cloaked figure.

There are reports of taps that won't turn off, a giggling girl in the deserted cellar and furniture flipping over by itself.

Occasionally ghost-hunters come to spend the night in the bar, in the hope of being spooked, as they have done at the **West Riding** in Wellington Street, where many strange noises and curious goings-on which have been reported over the years.

Armley's **Royal Hotel** is reputedly haunted by the mistress of a landlord who murdered her in Victorian times; Addingham's **Swan** by a coachman, a girl and a dog; the yard- thick limestone walls of Ledston's **White Horse** are home to an array of ghosts who scatter toilet rolls after dark. The long-dead landlord of the **Old Tree** at Kippax is an occasionally mischievous presence.

At the **Scotts Arms** in Sicklinghall you can choose your spectral company. One table is regularly visited by a pair of ancient gravediggers, another by a couple who died of TB a century ago. A milkmaid, a blacksmith's daughter and a soldier make up the full complement of spiritual inhabitants. Several mediums have visited and confirmed an identical roll call, apparently.

The **White House** at Oakwood has a ghostly girl who runs along a corridor late at night, a door that slams itself – and so many noises in the attic that the owners once called in Rentokil. They found nothing ●

soon owned by the dye plant next door, chiefly so they could regulate the drinking habits of the workforce. For those of us who prefer more mainstream entertainment, the Abbey remains a popular music venue. Around the walls are clarinets, guitars, a trombone and a mini drumkit. On one wall a bodhrán has been decorated with an advertisement for Tuesday's acoustic nights. But the main attractions will always be the sensible, sturdy, traditional pub food and quality real ale.

Doubtless the host of guest ales which jostle for attention against Martin's two regulars, refreshing Leeds Pale and citric Mary Jane, were a key factor in that timely CAMRA award.

Bar and brasserie: The Town Street Tavern is now warm and welcoming

Town Street Tavern

Town Street, Horsforth, LS18 4RJ.
☎ **0113 281 9996**
www.markettowntaverns.co.uk

A CHANGE of management has seen the Town Street Tavern revive local interest in its food. The bar itself was doing well – its eclectic selection of real ales, craft beers and interesting continental lagers proving as popular as ever – but the brasserie was losing trade: "It felt empty and cold, unfriendly and unwelcoming," says boss Dave Fleming, installed with a brief to revive its restaurant trade.

The opportunity to join Market Town Taverns and lead the development of one of its flagship houses was one that he jumped at.

Horsforth house: *Town Street Tavern is a flagship enterprise*

The commitment to great real ale is a company hallmark and here there are eight.

While four are changing guests, including at least one dark beer, four are permanent fixtures, including Okell's Bitter from

Horsforth pub crawl

EFFECTIVELY bisected by the ring road, Horsforth sprawls north towards Cookridge and south towards Kirkstall and the Hawksworth estate.

While there are some decent pubs within the suburb's southern portion – not least the excellent **Bridge** at the foot of Butcher Hill, it is the area outside the ring road which offers the greater opportunity for a pub crawl.

You could start at the **Fox &** **Hounds** beside Horsforth railway station. Though part of the food-led Ember Inn chain, the Fox offers a decent selection of real ales. From here you could wander to the **Old Ball**, recently reinvented as a pizza kitchen, and from there it's a short hop to the **Brownlee Arms**, a gastropub named in honour of the suburb's Olympic heroes.

Then there is the short walk down gently sloping Town Street where venues such as **Bar 166,** the same Manx company which bought a controlling interest in MTT a few years ago.

Pump clips and beer mats around the walls show off the various real ales, predominantly from Yorkshire breweries, which have been on sale here in the past. There's an interesting bottled beer list as well, including BrewDog's notorious Tactical Nuclear Penguin (32% ABV), which is available in shot-glass measures. A short walk across the hardwood flooring from the front door brings you to a bar where plenty more beers, including a great choice of lagers, vie for your attention on the counter.

The decor is very simple – cream walls above sage green panelling, the furniture spartan wooden chairs, stools and benches. The strategic use of etched glass screens discreetly divides the main room into two, while a narrow beer garden to the side provides some welcome outdoor drinking space.

Bar meals are available here at lunchtimes, but – in common with a couple of the other MTT joints – the food menu broadens in the evenings when the upstairs brasserie offers its more comprehensive menu.

It's child and dog-friendly too.

Big value: Soak up the beer with a carvery on Leeds ring road, at the Woodside

The Great Leeds Pub Crawl

▌The Chemic Tavern

Johnston Street, Woodhouse, LS6 2NG.
☎ **0113 245 7670**
www.thechemictavern.co.uk

THAT Woodhouse is a true community was confirmed after a sharp increase in business rates put the Chemic under serious threat. Residents flocked to a hastily-arranged public meeting; within hours many had contributed to a crowdfunding bid to keep the pub afloat.

For the past two years The Chemic has been run by Robert Wood, Kate Riley and Charlotte Stanley, who took over when long-serving licensee Dawn Edwards called it a day. It operates on a shoestring: "There's no great cushion of money," says Robert. "Once all the bills and wages have been paid, we have about £60 a week profit to put back into the pub." Which was manageable, until their council rates bill went up by £2,500.

"The response was insane. The public meeting was

Community favourite: The Bridge at the foot of Butcher Hill

Sandbar and **Medusa** compete for trade with the **Town Street Tavern** and lively sport–and–music venues the **Black Bull** and **Old King's Arms**.

At successive ring road junctions, the **Eleventh Earl** and **Woodside** pride themselves on their big-value carveries ●

*Last man
standing:
Robert Wood
outside the Chemic*

What's your poison: *The nearby chemical works once produced sulphuric acid*

packed, people started adding events to our calendar, and almost £1,000 was raised in the first 48 hours. We had people turn up who had never been in the pub before. One chap said that if we closed, he would have to move."

It's a measure both of the pub and of the community it serves. Dating back to the early 1800s, both pub and street take their names from the Johnston Chemical Works whose chief product was Vitriol – sulphuric acid – for the tanneries and dyeworks of the Meanwood Valley.

The area once had several pubs, but the Beer Exchange, Swan With Two Necks and wonderful old Bricklayers Arms have all been converted for housing, leaving the distinctive, stone-fronted Chemic as last one standing, though the resurgent Primrose on Meanwood Road is at last providing some competition.

The hashtag #onlyatthechemic celebrates that all of human life can be glimpsed here. Where else could you stumble upon a chap entertaining drinkers with his home-made clarinet, or a Breton music group, or a lipsync contest, which is essentially karaoke but without the singing?

The bar sits between the pub's two drinking spaces, offering a changing range of real ales. The airy front room, with its part-carpeted, part-flagged floor, has long tartan banquettes and attractive etched mirrors. The darker and more spartan back room is used for the array of functions and events; time is called by a very grand golden bell beside the bar.

The Chemic stands right at the centre of Woodhouse life, as much the focus for life in this inner-city community as it was in its sulphuric past.

Etched mirrors: *The Chemic is a welcome sight*

Legacy maintained: Matt Lovatt and Juan Mendoza continue to produce highly popular beers at a brewery established by the late Simon Bolderson

Ridgeside Brewery

BREWERS Matt Lovatt and Juan Mendoza took over at Ridgeside Brewery in August 2015, and are now charged with the duty of maintaining the legacy of the late great Simon Bolderson.

Simon loved his beer – and invested that passion along with his money and engineering experience into setting up the brewery in modest premises in Meanwood Road, a short walk from the Chemic, in 2010.

When Simon died four years later aged just 46 after a brave battle with cancer, Rawdon Crematorium was packed for his funeral. A variety of magazine articles and beer blogs each spoke of a wonderful man, taken cruelly young.

But perhaps the greatest tribute, and the one of which he'd be most proud, is the fact that his brewery is thriving and his own beers are continuing to sell.

Gently refreshing Cascade pale ale (4.1%), big-tasting fruity Coda IPA (5.7%) and dark, spicy porter Black Night (5%) were all Simon's recipes and remain at the heart of the business plan for the new regime ●

Brudenell Social Club

Queens Road, LS6 1NY.
☎ **0113 275 2411**
www.brudenellsocialclub.co.uk

HEMMED in by terraced housing in the tight-knit streets of Burley, the phenomenon that is the Brudenell is the busiest social club in the city, run by its members as a not-for-profit organisation and drawing in beer lovers and those attracted to its wide-ranging music programme.

There are live acts on almost every night, with music of every style and persuasion. Even big-name bands like Franz Ferdinand and Kaiser Chiefs have been known to turn up here to perform 'secret' gigs in this intimate fan-shaped venue.

Yet unlike most clubs where music is king, the Brudenell is also proud of its beers, serving a fine range of cask and craft

Secret gigs: Brudenell Social Club is well-known for hosting big name live acts

Electric nights:
Eli 'Paperboy' Reed
entertains at the
Brudenell

ales, while snooker, pool, darts and Sky TV add to its menu of attractions.

The club was founded in 1913 and its name is inextricably linked with the events of 25 October 1854, when the Seventh Earl of Cardigan led the ill-fated Charge of the Light Brigade at the Battle of Balaclava.

By this time, there had been a Cardigan Arms in Burley Road for 50 years, taking its name from local landowners the Earls of Cardigan, whose family name was Brudenell. The Seventh Earl had enjoyed a chequered career both as an army officer and politician during which time he displayed incompetence and simple generosity in roughly equal measure.

Whether he misunderstood, or whether it was deliberately miscommunicated, Cardigan displayed immense bravery to lead the Light Brigade's charge. He did so with the resigned cry: "Here goes the last of the Brudenells," careering headlong down the 'Valley of Death' into the teeth of the Russian guns. More than one hundred died, yet remarkably, Cardigan survived.

Light Brigade:
The Cardigan Arms
in Burley Road

Members' clubs

HALF a mile from the Brudenell, New Burley Club offers another great example of a private members' club.

In many ways it operates like a community pub, opening its doors to the locals and providing everything they need by way of entertainment. Here that means three-times-weekly bingo sessions, live music, tango classes, line-dancing, country and western nights.

A peppercorn annual membership fee gives you access to cheap beer, snooker tables and a reliably sociable atmosphere.

This winning combination has allowed many private members' clubs continue to survive, even in areas where pubs themselves have struggled and closed.

Leeds has plenty. Some were founded as a place for politics – the Conservative Clubs, Labour Clubs and Liberal Clubs. Many gave colleagues a chance to socialise together, whether at career-specific venues like the Post Office Club or Ex-Servicemen's Clubs, or at WMCs, open to all.

I remain a member of the much loved Yorkshire Post Sports and Social Club which survives just as a bowls team. Our clubhouse was sadly

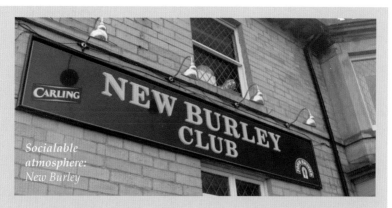

Socialable atmosphere: New Burley

never rebuilt following an arson attack some years ago.

Other clubs are devoted to sport or music and draw diehard regulars who see these places as a daily feature of their lives.

I've enjoyed beer tastings at Adel Sports and Social Club, parties at Old Leos in Adel, and nights of jazz at Armley Conservative Club. Visit www.leedssocialclubs.co.uk for a list of plenty more ●

The Hungry Bear

Stonegate Road, Meanwood, LS6 4HY.
☎ 0113 274 0241
www.thehungrybear.co.uk

IF there were a single bar that epitomised the transformation of Leeds as a drinking and dining destination, this would be it.

Though primarily a restaurant, the Hungry Bear serves a dazzling range of beers created in its own one-room brewhouse upstairs.

Owner James Coupland moved here from the midlands, and after spells at noted establishments such as the Wood Hall Hotel at Wetherby and the Box Tree at Ilkley, set up the Hungry Bear in 2013. He enlisted pal Phil Marsh, who's in charge of the beers, which are brewed in 90-litre batches and decanted into the bottles.

The Great Leeds Pub Crawl

You could swing a cat in the brewhouse, but not a very large one.

When you order beer, it's served by the bottle, and I was impressed by the dark, smoky, chocolately Flying Bells Porter (4.5% ABV) which has a really dusty, papery aftertaste, redolent of musty old books. It might sound odd, but that's a really lovely finish.

Outback IPA (4.5%) gains its cocktail of peach, melon, apricot and passion fruit from Australian Galaxy hops.

The beers are the perfect accompaniment to the quality food which James produces for the first floor restaurant; staff are happy to suggest appropriate food and beer pairings.

Meanwood and Far Headingley

THE success of the **Hungry Bear** is perhaps the most potent symbol of Meanwood's resurgence as a drinking destination, yet it joined a marketplace where two excellent bars were already thriving.

East of Arcadia, Market Town Taverns' first 'new build' pub, *right,* opened in 2010 and provided an immediate outlet for the nascent Ridgeside Brewery which had been established nearby.

Next to arrive was the smaller **Alfred**, which brought North Bar's cosmopolitan beers and quirky decor to a suburb where a giant Waitrose was a significant symbol of regeneration.

A brisk walk in either direction provides some further alternatives. Heading west, you will quickly arrive at Far Headingley, where some serious

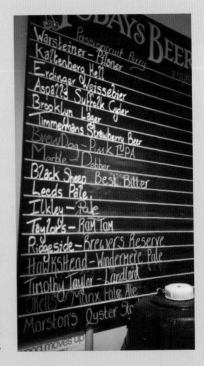

Lots of bottle: The Hungry Bear's dazzling range

A few years ago, this cultured, enlightened combination of high-end cuisine and micro-brewed ales might even have struggled in the trendiest city centre location. That it can now thrive in a suburb once dominated by the soulless Meanwood Arms and dangerous Beckett's is truly astonishing.

investment has seen Greene King transform Woodies into a really interesting craft alehouse, and the **Three Horsehoes**, *right*, has shaken off an era of disrepute to re-emerge as a proper local serving decent food and drink.

Just along the road, the **New Inn** is another popular Greene King House. Around the corner is **Beer Ritz**, a fabulous specialist off-licence stocked from floor to ceiling with beers from around the globe.

Walk north instead and you'll soon reach Meanwood's longer established community pubs, the lively **Bay Horse** and the real ale haven of the **Myrtle Tavern**, which has been thoroughly revived by manager Scott Westlake after some sad years of decline ●

The Great Leeds Pub Crawl

Further North

Harrogate Road, Chapel Allerton, LS7 4NZ.
☎ **0113 237 0962**
www.northbar.com/further-north

FOR years now, Further North has been my end-of-week venue of choice, as my mate Gareth and I pick over the embers of another five days at work, and set the world to rights in time for the weekend.

It's a ritual played out in pubs and bars of all descriptions across the world, and it just happens that we choose to observe it in Further North.

That it's in roughly equal walking distance from our respective homes is the reason we came here in the first place; that it offers reliable beer and a really sociable atmosphere are why we stayed.

Aladdin's cave:
Further North

If you're driving anywhere near 30mph up Harrogate Road, you will almost certainly miss it. In my youth, this was the poky little Rally and Speed Shop, an Aladdin's cave of spare bulbs and spraypaints. If you ever needed a windscreen wiper assembly for a 1979 Austin Allegro, this was the place to come. North Bar took a great leap of faith by converting it into a bar, in a suburb already adequately served by licensed premises.

Though constrained by geometry, they wrought a remarkable conversion, making its lack of size a virtue – and creating with interesting photographs and an eccentric selection of lampshades a quirky little bolthole quite distinct from the more glitzy bars of the suburb's main circuit.

Stepping in from busy Harrogate Road, you enter beside

a tiny L-shaped bar with just two handpumps, the first invariably Protoype, originally from Kirkstall Brewery but now made by the newly-established North Brewing Co. Fonts dispense craft ales and quality lagers while fridges are stocked with an eclectic range that quite belies the size of this tiny venue.

On winter nights when we're propping up the bar, or on warm evenings, when they draw back the long glass sliding doors and we're almost sitting on the pavement, there's nowhere I'd rather be.

Chapel Allerton

THE development of Chapel Allerton as a desirable postcode and night-time destination is one of the more remarkable changes Leeds has experienced in the past two decades.

Those keen to bar-hop can enjoy a lively circuit starting at the **Queen's** on Harrogate Road. Its current Toby Carvery branding is just the latest guise for a pub which has been a plug-in-and-play space for the marketing whizzkids who have shaped it as an Ember Inn, a Wacky Warehouse, a Real Macaw – and was once a Tetley's Cavalier Steakhouse.

After **Further North**, you can nip into Regent Street for the real ale venue **Regent** and down Hawthorn Road for the more down-at-heel **Nag's Head**.

From here, head back to the Stainbeck Lane junction and enjoy a little tour around **Pit**, **Kith and Kin** and the lively **Manor**. On summer evenings, drinkers spill out onto the

Kirkstall Bridge Inn

Bridge Road, Kirkstall, LS5 3BW.
☎ **0113 278 4044**
www.kirkstallbridge.co.uk

FOR years known as the Old Bridge, this famous old pub has been renamed to reference both its location and ownership.

It sits right beside the west Leeds suburb's busy River Aire

Remarkable changes: Real ale can be found in the Regent, left, and a sunny – or summer's evening – patio awaits at the Pit, near Stainbeck Lane junction

pavement patios of each of these, lending a continental feel to a suburb which has utterly reinvented itself.

There's the lovely old **Mustard Pot**, with its quality food, excellent choice of real ales, and wonderful sun–trap beer garden, and the recently re-opened **Woods**. Further down Harrogate Road is the splendid **Seven Arts**, which does good food and hand–pulled ale – plus an eclectic range of music, drama, film and comedy in its intimate rear theatre space.

Our tour ends a little further down at the **Three Hulats**, which supplies everything you would demand from a Wetherspoon pub ●

crossing, ideally placed to attract passing traffic on the routes between Stanningley, Bramley and Headingley. It re-opened in 2013 after a lengthy refit carried out by owners Kirkstall Brewery, whose premises are a short walk away, just beyond the Leeds-Liverpool Canal.

In less than two years it has garnered an enviable clutch of accolades, including a national award from English Heritage as the best refurbishment in the country and been twice named Leeds CAMRA's Pub of the Year.

Though it's not nearly as old as the nearby abbey, stepping inside the Kirkstall Bridge is to enter a pub where tradition is clearly prized. From the car park, you enter an intimate downstairs bar of simple furniture and wooden panelling. A stairway leads to the pub's upper bar at roadside level where the same theme continues. Every wall is hung with posters, mirrors and advertisements, where great companies from the history of brewing are celebrated –

KIRKSTALL BRIDGE

Leeds CAMRA Pub of the year - again! 2014 & 2015

KIRKSTALL
NERY

Clutch of accolades:
Kirkstall Bridge Inn
has twice been named
CAMRA Pub of the Year

The Great Leeds Pub Crawl

Allsopps IPA, Ind Coope, Cains Superior Ales and Bass Burton Ales. Further displays echo the beery theme.

Some quality food is served most sessions, including a black pudding and chorizo pizza if you're feeling adventurous. "We also do the best Sunday roast in Leeds," says manager Ian Forster. "The Cross Keys do a good one, but ours is better."

Smile for CAMRA: Ian Forster receives his award from Mike Hampshire

Kirkstall Brewery

THE Kirkstall Bridge is essentially Kirkstall Brewery's tap, a place where they can showcase their cask and keg ales alongside some interesting guests.

The brewery grew out of the Vertical Drinks business, best known for being first to import the fabulous Sierra Nevada ales to the UK, and boss Steve Holt remains as passionate as ever about introducing British customers to new tastes from overseas.

Vertical will shortly be moving horizontally along Kirkstall Road, where the facilities of an abandoned dairy and refrigerated trucks will be ideal for ensuring that beers from the likes of Firestone Walker in California, Odell in Colorado, Edge in Barcelona and Italy's Birrificio Italiano reach customers in perfect condition.

The brewery's own products are becoming an increasingly popular sight on bars across the city,

Spoilt for choice:
Horse & Farrier

Otley Pub Crawl

with their biggest seller being the the pale and hoppy Three Swords (4.5%). Their entry-level ale is the very sessionable Kirkstall Pale (4%) while the dark and full-bodied Black Band Porter (5.5%) and lovely golden Dissolution IPA (5%) complete the regular range.

In bottle, the stronger Dissolution Extra IPA, *pictured left*, is fabulous. Its name evokes the turbulent time towards the end of the reign of Henry VIII, when the Cistercian monks of Kirkstall were forced to surrender their beautiful abbey to the crown. The Kirkstall Bridge is just a couple of hundred yards from the ruins, which are well worth a visit ●

FOR years, Otley has been well served by its enviable variety of pubs; the explosion in the popularity of real ale and the emergence of exciting ale bars and micro-breweries has taken that to fresh heights. It's probably coincidence that its MP should be the beer loving, pub campaigning Greg Mulholland, but it doesn't do any harm.

Just a quick wander around the town centre brings you to a host of places

I MM 1755

The **OLD COCK**

INDEPENDENT
FREE HOUSE

STRICTLY NO
UNDER 18
WAITING
UPSTAIRS
DOGS
WELCOME
NO DRINKS
OUTSIDE

THE
OLD COCK

GOOD BEER
GOOD CHEER

ALWAYS ON TAP HERE

Author's favourite
Otley's Old Cock

worth visiting, and our trail starts at the **Fleece** in Westgate, an ancient pub once known as the Golden Fleece and now beautifully restored. Heading towards the town centre, we reach the cosy one-roomed **Cross Pipes**, before arriving at the 17th century **Black Horse**, reckoned by some to be the finest building in Otley. It's a hotel too, with nine letting bedrooms.

From here it's a short hop to the Market Place and two fine old boozers – the **Bay Horse** and **Black Bull**. The latter is the oldest pub in the town and has the proud boast of having been drunk dry by Cromwell's troops, before they made similarly short work of the Royalists at Marston Moor. Nearby in Boroughgate is the excellent **Otley Tap House**, a brand new addition to the scene and fresh competition for the **White Swan** next door.

Beside each other in Kirkgate, the **Red Lion** and **Whitaker's** are lively traditional ale houses, while tucked away in Newmarket is the old Ring O' Bells, now given a fresh lease of life as the **Otley Tavern**.

A walk along Bondgate could start at **North Bar Social**, the Leeds bar company's most northern outlet, before we reach the **Bowling Green** which is doing great business as a Wetherspoons – the glass roof over a central courtyard creates a bright and airy place to drink.

Further along is the sturdy, stone-fronted **Rose and Crown**, which generally attracts a slightly older crowd, before we reach **Korks** wine bar, which manages the neat trick of combining great live music with quality food, and the fine real ale venue **The Junction**. The **Manor** in Walkergate is a Thwaites pub, well known for live music.

Good business: *The Bowling Green and, right, the revitalised Otley Tavern*

Otley Breweries

IT's perfectly fitting that a town with such a great array of pubs should also boast a brace of great small breweries.

Established in 2005, **Rodham's** is now well established after starting life in a one-barrel plant in Michael Rodham's cellar.

Capacity has gradually increased and Rodham's beers are worth trying, when they can be found, which is sadly not that often.

I've enjoyed a pint of Michael's really firm and assertive hoppy IPA in the past, and my occasional drinking buddy Leigh Linley recommends his smoky Albion Porter – but it's a pleasure I have yet to enjoy.

The Old Cock often serves ales from **Briscoe's**, another which started on a tiny brew kit in the owner's cellar – and has been there ever since, barring a brief stint away in a local pub. Briscoe's are not afraid to experiment and have brewed in many styles from light hoppy bitters through stouts to strong ales.

Otley Beer Festival, held every November, offers another chance to check out these two popular local brews ●

The Great Leeds Pub Crawl

But we'll finish at my favourite Otley pub, the **Old Cock** in Crossgate. The building dates back to 1751, but the pub is little more than five years old. Even so, it has established itself as a firm favourite on the local scene, and has won countless CAMRA awards for its beers.

Fine old boozer: The Black Bull in Otley...

An inviting line of nine real ale handpulls dominate the long bar which is dead ahead as you cross the threshold; continental alternatives such as Leffe, Hoegaarden and Kaltenberg play to the Europhiles.

For a comprehensive list of pubs, including a few more just outside the town centre, visit www.otleypubclub.co.uk

Collingham Brewery

WETHERBY's nearest brewery is at Collingham – and I first encountered its excellent sessionable Journeyman ale (3.9%) at the **Lord Darcy**, a sizeable pub and family restaurant in Harrogate Road at Moortown.

After enjoying this well-balanced Yorkshire best bitter, I sought out their other flagship ale, the distinguished hoppy Artisan's Choice pale ale (4.4%), which was a winner at York's beer festival in 2012.

Seasonal specials add to the range, outlets such as **The Atlas** (p76) and **Preston** in Oakwood are regular stockists.

Wetherby Pub Crawl

THE LS22 postcode is huge, stretching almost to Tockwith in the east and Harewood in the west. This pub crawl concentrates on the pubs around the centre of its biggest town, and starts on North Street, with the traditional **Royal Oak**, which has a lovely beer garden and guest bedrooms to complement its selection of real ales and good value food.

Further along is the curiously-named **Swan & Talbot**. Once a welcome halt for travellers on the Great North Road, it has recently upped its game with some really top-notch food.

Turning into Westgate we come to **Muse**, which offers the tried and tested food-ale-and-atmosphere formula of the Market Town Taverns group, before we reach the busy **New Inn**, which strives to be all things to all people, combining a good choice of beers with a remarkable cosmopolitan menu – and Sky Sports.

Stone-fronted: ...and its Yorkshire-loving namesake up the road in Wetherby

The Great Leeds Pub Crawl

Their own dry, bitter and refreshing New Inn Pale Ale is certainly worth a try.

We enter the north side of the ancient Market Place to reach the stone-fronted **Black Bull**, which makes a great play of its Yorkshire-dominated real ales. From here it's a short hop to **Bar Three**, which offers bistro-style food and a small selection of ales.

Author favourite: In Wetherby that honour goes to the Crown Inn

We cross the road to the High Street and two further lively live sport pubs, the **Red Lion**, which is in Position-A for drinkers entering the town across its bridge, and the **Brunswick**.

But the modest utilitarian little pub in between is perhaps my favourite in Wetherby.

The **Crown** is a two-roomed Sam Smith's house, whose pale yellow decor, tiled fireplaces, wooden back bar, floral patterned carpet, stained glass and frosted lanterns look just as they might have done in the 1950s.

The familiar choice of the Tadcaster brewery's own cask and keg beers pale into insignificance against some of the other bars in the town, but the wonderful unspoiled atmosphere more than compensates.

Wetherby pub crawl: Bistro-style Bar Three, the widely appealing New Inn...

...the Brunswick in the High Street and the Royal Oak, beer garden and all

Acknowledgements

FOR their encouragement I owe a lasting debt of gratitude to the great and good of British beer writing, many of whom I am privileged to count as friends, including Roger Protz, Barrie Pepper, Pete Brown, Sophie Atherton, Marverine Cole, Mark Fletcher, Des De Moor, Leigh Linley, Jerry Bartlett and Adrian Tierney-Jones. Each of them writes staggeringly well; their varied influences can be felt throughout this book.

I remain grateful to the late Michael Jackson who proved a critical friend early in my career.

Equally I am grateful to those who have joined me on the various expeditions needed to assemble this guide, and who suffered in silence as I wrote my scratchy little notes. My wife Katrina and our grown-up children Ben and Hannah deserve special mention for putting up with my disappearances – either to the pub or to my study to write.

Thanks to Sam Moss at Leeds Brewery for his support, and to Tony Hannan and Phil Caplan at Scratching Shed Publishing for their encouragement to produce a second edition of this book, putting behind me the disappointment I felt when the publishers of the 2011 edition went into liquidation, leaving me significantly out of pocket.

Thanks also to Jonny Brown of the *YEP* and Amy Crumpton of Pink Gorilla for their helpful suggestions of the best new bars on the scene.

I am grateful to my colleagues past and present – Sue Underwood, David Garth, Nick East, Chris Bunting, Leigh Marklew, Ben and Rachel Oldham, Paul Robinson and Gareth Dant – who shared the burden of proof-reading, and to the talented Mark Bickerdike for once again helping out with some last-minute photographs.

Picture Credits

I AM grateful to those many people who helped me to assemble the photographs for this second edition of the *Great British Pub Crawl*.

Those on pages 10, 16, 21, 22 (left), 24, 27 (right), 31 (above), 39 (below), 42, 45, 56-7, 63-4, 66 (below), 71 (above), 74, 91, 98, 103, 108, 121, 124, 137 (below right), 140 (below), 152 (above), 154, 156 (above), 160, 163 (above), 168, 169 (below), 174, 178 (below), 211, 214 and 221-2 appear by courtesy of Yorkshire Post Newspapers – and I remain grateful to Paul Napier, Andy Manning, Keith Hampshire, Ian Day and David Clay for allowing me access to the picture archive there.

The amazing Refectory music images (page 172) were by my old friends Dave Siviour and Steve "Fritz" Riding, and appear by courtesy of the University of Leeds, where there is a permanent exhibition of the work of these two great veteran music snappers.

Perhaps not quite at the veteran stage of his career, former *YEP* photographer Mark Bickerdike's talents can be seen throughout this book. I'm grateful for his efforts in providing the pictures for pages 5, 15, 17, 23, 107, 109, 128-30, 138, 140 (above), 142-3, 146-7, 149, 164-7, 170, 181 and 193-5.

The Leeds International Beer Festival (p140-1) images are by another talented *YEP* man James Hardisty, Ridgeside Brewery (p220) by beer writer David "Bloke From Hull" Litten and Whippet Brewery (p103) by Tony Johnson, arguably Britain's leading pumpclip photographer.

Several bars and PR companies were kind enough to provide images too. The interior images of the Town Hall Tavern (p159) and of pub food (p137 below left) are courtesy of Chocolate PR; pictures of MOJO (p196, 198, 199 right) and Oporto (p88-89) are by courtesy of Sharon Brigden at SLBPR.

North Bar (p67 and p203-4), Further North (p229) and Preston (p67) appear by courtesy of North Bar Group. Call Lane Social (p82, p90) and cocktails (p96, p99) are by John Tudor.

The pictures of Tapped (p114, 131-3, 137 (above) and 152 (below)) appear with the kind permission of the Tapped Brew Co, while the old picture of the Pack Horse (p176) was loaned by landlord Paul McIntyre.

Belgrave (p9 and p183-5) are by Tom Joy and Bundobust (p115-116) by Giles Smith. Both these sets appear courtesy of Simon Fogal of I Like Press Ltd.

The remainder of the images, including the maps, were by the author, with the single exception of the picture in the centre of the right-hand column of p169 which was taken by a very drunken Ben Jenkins, dressed as Buddy Holly, on his 18th birthday pub crawl. Make-up by Hannah Jenkins.

Bibliography and Further Reading

TO a greater or lesser degree, each of these books has assisted my preparation of *The Great Leeds Pub Crawl*, both this edition and the 2011 original – and in my gradual understanding of pubs, of beers, of the great British pub culture and of local history:

Yorkshire's Real Heritage Pubs edited by David Gamston (*CAMRA Books*)

Fifty Great Pub Crawls by Barrie Pepper (*CAMRA Books*)

Old Inns and Pubs of Leeds by Barrie Pepper (*Alewords*)

Real Ale in Central Leeds edited by Adrian Rankin (*CAMRA Books*)

The Leeds Pub Trail Compendium edited by Mark Firth (*CAMRA Books*)

The Oxford Companion to Beer edited by Garrett Oliver (*Oxford University Press*)

300 Beers To Try Before You Die by Roger Protz (*CAMRA Books*)

Great Yorkshire Bottled Beer by Leigh Linley (*Great Northern*)

Great British Pubs by Adrian Tierney-Jones (*CAMRA Books*)

Local history: The Fleece in Otley

Twenty First Century Leeds – Geographies of a Regional City, edited by Rachael Unsworth and John Stillwell (*Leeds University Press*)

Leeds – Pevsner Architectural Guide by Susan Wrathmell (*Yale University Press*)

Leeds Old and New by Percy Robinson (*Richard Jackson Limited*)

Far Headingley, Weetwood and West Park by David Hall (*Far Headingley Village Society*)

Chapel Allerton – from village to suburb by R Faulkner (*Chapel Allerton Residents Association*)

The Knights Templar in Yorkshire by Diane Holloway and Trish Colton (*The History Press*)

Index

Index

The Great Leeds Pub Crawl

Water's edge: *Pour House in the Cradle of Industry*

The Great Leeds Pub Crawl

Trainspotting: The balcony at the Brewery Tap on the Station Circuit

LEEDS
BREWERY

18 New Station Street,
Leeds, LS1 5DL
E: info@brewerytapleeds.co.uk
W: brewerytapleeds.co.uk
T: 0113 243 4414

101 Water Lane,
Leeds, LS11 5QN
E: info@midnightbell.co.uk
W: midnightbell.co.uk
T: 0113 244 5044

Swan Street,
Leeds, LS1 6LG
E: info@whiteswanleeds.co.uk
W: whiteswanleeds.co.uk
T: 0113 242 0187

King's Square
York, YO1 8BH
e: info@lbdukeofyork.com
w: www.lbdukeofyork.com
t: 01904 676 065

4-12 Harper Street
Leeds, LS2 7EA
e: info@crowdoffavours.co.uk
w: www.crowdoffavours.co.uk
t: 0113 246 9405

1 Church Row
Leeds, LS2 7HD
e: info@lambandflagleeds.co.uk
w: www.lambandflagleeds.co.uk
t: 0113 243 1255

www.leedsbrewery.co.uk